The Object Database Standard: ODMG-93

The Object Database Standard: ODMG-93

Edited by
R.G.G. Cattell

With contributions by

Tom Atwood
Joshua Duhl
Guy Ferran
Mary Loomis
Drew Wade

Morgan Kaufmann Publishers
San Mateo, California

Senior Editor: Bruce M. Spatz
Production Manager: Yonie Overton
Assistant Editor: Douglas Sery
Copyeditor: Fran Taylor
Cover Design: Patty King
Proofreader: Judy Weiss
Printer: Edwards Brothers, Inc.

This book has been author-typeset using Framemaker.

Editorial Offices:
Morgan Kaufmann Publishers
2929 Campus Drive, Suite 260
San Mateo, CA 94403

97 96 95 94 5 4 3 2 1

Library of Congress Cataloging-in-Publication Data

The Object database standard, ODMG-93 / edited by R.G.G. Cattell ;
with contributions by Tom Atwood . . . [et al.].
p. cm.
Includes index.
ISBN 1-55860-302-6
1. Object-orinted data bases—Standards. I. Cattell, R. G. G.
(Roderick Geoffrey Galton) II. Atwood, Tom.
QA76.9.D3024 1994
005.75—dc20 93-32235
CIP

Contents

Preface

This book is intended for programmers, end-users, managers, students, and researchers interested in a standard for object database management systems. The ODMG-93 standard described in this book is the result of many man-years of work, with contributions from many companies. Implementations of ODMG-93 are promised in as little as a year from now, so this book should be useful in development, research, planning, and better understanding the direction of the industry.

Please keep in mind that this document represents work in progress. It is by no means perfect; errors will be discovered and corrected as work progresses. There are known shortcomings that we have deferred to future work. Nevertheless, we felt it important to get wider feedback and implementation experience with the standard, rather than further delay release of the specification while we refine it in a small group. Since ODMG is currently not a formal standards body, and it has no office for copying or distribution of this document, we are publishing the specification as a book to make it easily accessible.

If you want the latest information on the status of the ODMG standards proposal (in order to find out when and how future releases will be available), or if you have corrections or suggestions, please see the ODMG email address at the top of page 9.

Thanks are due to many people for helping in this endeavor; these contributors are listed in Chapter 1.

Rick Cattell
August 1, 1993

Agenda
RFI
ODL
OML
OQL
next meetings

Chapter 1

Overview

1.1 Background

This document describes the results of over a year's work toward standards for object database management systems (ODBMSs) undertaken by the members of the Object Database Management Group (ODMG). Our proposal represents a substantial creative effort that we believe will significantly change the object database industry.

We chose to work outside of traditional standards bodies for our efforts in order to make quick progress. Standards groups are well suited to incremental changes to a proposal once a good starting point has been established, but it is difficult to perform substantial creative work in such organizations due to their lack of continuity, large membership, and infrequent meetings. It should be noted that relational database standards started with a database model and language implemented by the largest company involved (IBM); for our work, we have picked and combined the best features of half a dozen implementations we had available to us.

1.1.1 Importance of a Standard

To date, the lack of a standard for object databases has been a major limitation to their more widespread use. The success of relational database systems did not result simply from a higher level of data independence and a simpler data model than previous systems. Much of their success came from the standardization that they offer. The acceptance of the SQL standard allows a high degree of portability and interoperability between systems, simplifies learning new relational DBMSs, and represents a wide endorsement of the relational approach.

All of these factors are important for object DBMSs, as well. In fact, these factors are even more important, because most of the products in this area are offered by young companies — portability and endorsement of the approach are essential to a customer. In addition, the scope of object DBMSs is more far-reaching than that of relational DBMSs, integrating the programming language and database system, and encompassing all of an application's operations and data. A standard is critical to making such applications practical.

So, for the success of the object database industry, standards are overdue. The intense ODMG effort has given the object database industry a "jump start" toward standards that would otherwise have taken many years. ODMG enables many vendors to support and endorse a common object database interface to which customers write their applications.

1.1.2 Goals

Our primary goal is to put forward a set of standards allowing an ODBMS customer to write portable applications, i.e., applications that could run on more than one ODBMS product. The data schema, programming language binding, and data manipulation and query languages must be portable. Eventually, we hope our standards proposal will be helpful in allowing interoperability between the ODBMS products, as well, e.g., for heterogeneous distributed databases communicating through the OMG Object Request Broker.

We are striving to bring programming languages and database systems to a new level of integration, moving the industry forward as a whole through the practical impetus of real products that conform to a more comprehensive standard than is possible with relational systems. We have gone further than the least common denominator of the first relational standards, and we want to provide portability for the entire application, not just the small portion of the semantics encoded in embedded SQL statements.

The ODMG member companies are committed to supporting this standard. Thus, we expect our proposal to become a de facto standard for this industry. We also plan to submit our proposal to standards groups for adoption. We recognize that our current draft needs to undergo further refinement and evolution, and this must happen in the standards arena.

We do not wish to produce identical ODBMS products. Our goal is source code portability; there is a lot of room for future innovation in a number of areas. There will be differences between products in performance, languages supported, functionality unique to particular market segments (e.g., version and configuration management), accompanying programming environments, application construction tools, small versus large scale, multithreading, networking, platform availability, depth of functionality, suites of predefined type libraries, GUI builders, design tools, and so on.

Wherever possible, we have used existing work as the basis for our proposals, from standards groups and from the literature. But, primarily, our work is derived by combining the strongest features of the ODBMS products currently available. These products offer demonstrated implementations of our standards components that have been tried in the field.

1.1.3 Definition

It is important to define the scope of our efforts, since ODBMSs provide an architecture that is significantly different than other DBMSs — they are a revolutionary rather than an evolutionary development. Rather than providing only a high-level language such as SQL for data manipulation, an ODBMS transparently integrates database capability with the application programming language. This transparency makes it unnecessary to learn a separate DML, obviates the need to explicitly copy and translate data between database and programming language representations, and supports substantial performance advantages through data caching in applications. The ODBMS includes the query language capability of relational systems as well, and the query language model is more powerful, e.g., it incorporates lists and arrays as well as sets.

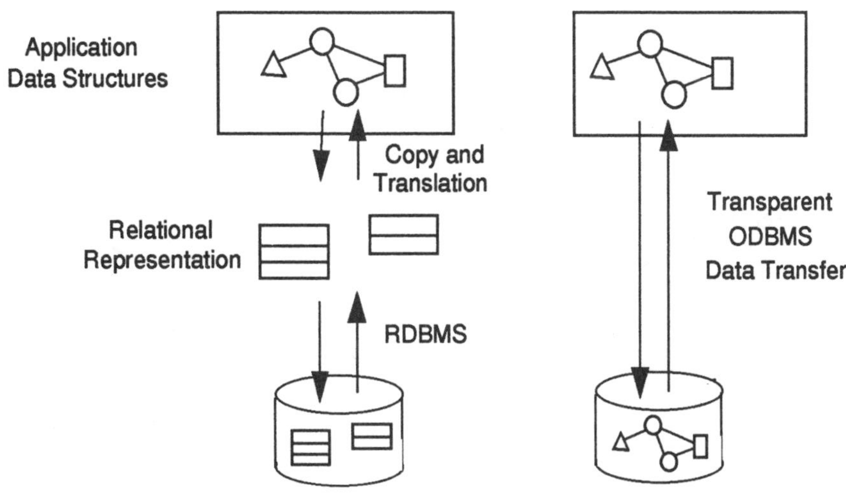

Figure 1-1. Comparison of DBMS Architectures

In summary, we define an *ODBMS* to be a DBMS that integrates database capabilities with object-oriented programming language capabilities. An ODBMS makes database objects appear as programming language objects, in one or more existing programming languages. The ODBMS extends the language with transparently persistent data, concurrency control, data recovery, associative queries, and other database capabilities. For more extensive definition and discussion of ODBMSs, the reader is referred to textbooks in this area (e.g., Cattell, *Object Data Management*).

In contrast to extended relational database systems, ODBMSs require standards based on integration with existing programming language syntax, semantics, and compilers. ODBMSs have been integrated with C++, C, Smalltalk, and LISP. There is some overlap with extended relational database systems, since we want our query language to retain some compatibility with the evolving SQL standard. However, the object paradigm must incorporate the entire application, not just embedded database statements, to be truly beneficial. In addition, 100% SQL compatibility greatly limits the clarity and power of an object query language. Therefore, we have balanced SQL compatibility with other aspirations.

1.2 Architecture

In order to understand the chapters of this book, it is necessary to understand the overall architecture of ODBMSs.

1.2.1 Major Components

The major components of our standard are described in subsequent chapters of the book:

Object Model. The common data model to be supported by ODBMSs is described in Chapter 2. We have used the OMG Object Model as the basis for our model. The OMG core model was designed to be a common denominator for object request brokers, object database systems, object programming languages, and other applications. In keeping with the OMG Architecture, we have designed an ODBMS *profile* for their model, adding components (e.g., relationships) to the OMG core object model to support our needs.

Object Definition Language. The data definition language for ODBMSs is described in Chapter 3. We call this the object definition language, or ODL, to distinguish it from traditional database data definition languages, or DDLs. We use the OMG interface definition language (IDL) as the basis for ODL syntax.

Object Query Language. We define a declarative (nonprocedural) language for querying and updating database objects. This object query language, or OQL, is described in Chapter 4. We have used the relational standard SQL as the basis for OQL, where possible, though OQL must support more powerful capabilities. We have not used the extended relational standard in progress, SQL3, because of limitations in its data model and because of its historical "baggage." However, we hope that OQL and SQL3 can converge at a future date.

C++ Language Binding. The most important programming language for ODBMSs has proven to be C++. Chapter 5 discusses the standard binding of ODBMSs to C++; it explains how to write portable C++ code that manipulates persistent objects. This is called the C++ OML, or object manipulation language. The C++ binding also includes a version of the ODL that uses C++ syntax, a mechanism to invoke OQL, and procedures for operations on databases and transactions.

Smalltalk Language Binding. We have also drafted an ODBMS binding for Smalltalk, to support applications for which that is the most appropriate programming language. It is possible to read and write the same database from both Smalltalk and C++, as long as the programmer stays within the common subset of supported data types.

More chapters may be added at a future date for other language bindings, such as Pascal, LISP, and IDL. Note that unlike relational DBMSs, ODBMS data manipulation languages are tailored to specific application programming languages, in order to provide a single, integrated environment for programming and data manipulation. We don't believe exclusively in a universal DML syntax. We go further than relational systems, as we support a unified object model for sharing data across programming languages, as well as a common query language.

1.2.2 Additional Components

In addition to the object database standards, ODMG has produced some ancillary results aimed at forwarding the ODBMS industry. These have been included as appendices:

OMG Object Model Profile. Appendix A describes the differences between our object model and the OMG object model, so that Chapter 2 can stand alone. As just mentioned, we have defined the components in an ODBMS profile for OMG's model. This appendix delineates these components.

OMG ORB Binding. Appendix B describes how ODBMS objects could participate as OMG objects, through an adaptor to an object request broker (ORB) that routes object invocations through object identifiers provided by an ODBMS. We also outline the reverse: how ODBMSs can make use of the OMG ORB.

ANSI C++ Extension. Some minor extensions of ANSI C++ would greatly simplify the transparent integration of C++ wth ODBMSs. We describe these extensions in Appendix C.

1.2.3 ODBMS Architecture Perspective

A better understanding of the architecture of an ODBMS will help put the components we have discussed into perspective.

Figure 1-2 illustrates the use of the typical ODBMS product that we are trying to standardize. The programmer writes declarations for the application schema (both data and interfaces) plus a source program for the application implementation. The source program is written in a programming language (PL) such as C++, which has been extended to provide a full database OML including transactions, and object query. The schema declarations may be written in an extension of the programming language syntax, labeled PL ODL in the figure, or in a programming language-independent

ODL. The latter could be used as a higher-level design language, or to allow schema definition independent of programming language.

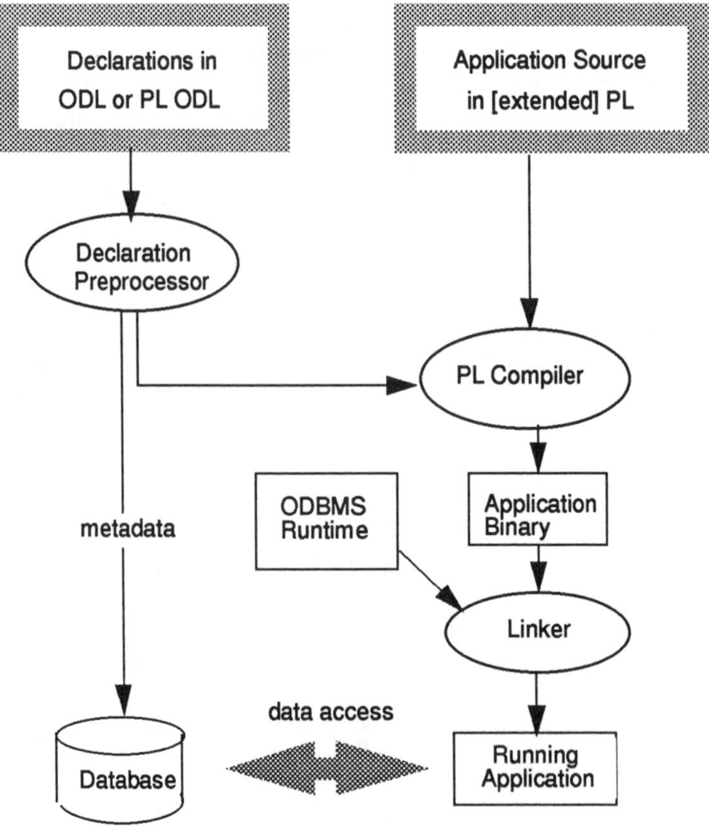

Figure 1-2: Using an ODBMS

The declarations and source program are then compiled and linked with the ODBMS to produce the running application. The application accesses a new or existing database, whose types must conform to the declarations. Databases may be shared with other applications on a network; the ODBMS provides a shared service for transaction and lock management, allowing data to be cached in the application.

1.3 Status

This document describes Version 1.0 of the ODMG standard, which we refer to as ODMG-93. The authors' companies are committed to support this standard.

1.3.1 Participants

The current participants in the ODMG are:

- Rick Cattell, chair, SunSoft
- Tom Atwood, member, Object Design
- Joshua Duhl, member, Ontos
- Guy Ferran, member, O_2 Technology
- Mary Loomis, member, Versant
- Drew Wade, member, Objectivity
- Jurgen Annevelink, reviewer, Hewlett-Packard
- Dirk Bartels, reviewer, Poet Software
- Jeff Galarneau, reviewer, Itasca
- Philippe Lelong, reviewer, Intellitic
- Mark Palmer, reviewer, Digital Equipment Corporation
- Jacob Stein, reviewer, Servio
- Craig Thompson, reviewer, Texas Instruments

It is to the personal credit of the ODMG voting members (who are also the authors of the ODMG-93 chapters that follow) that the first draft of this standard was produced so soon after the ODMG was formed. The members put substantial time and personal investment into the meetings and this document. They showed remarkable dedication to our goals; no one attempted to twist the process to his or her company's advantage. The reviewers were also very helpful, always ready to contribute. Given that we had no starting point from which to work, we could have taken years to develop and agree upon any one of the chapters in this book, yet the group moved quickly to all the results reported here.

Other individuals contributed to the text of this document in addition to the authors. Thanks are due to François Bancilhon from O_2 Technology on Chapter 4, Jacob Stein from Servio on Chapter 6, Bill Wilkinson from Objectivity on Chapter 5, and Phil Gust from Objectivity on Appendix B.

In addition to the regular ODMG participants above, we received valuable feedback from others in academia and industry. We would like to thank our academic reviewers Dave Maier, Dave Dewitt, Mike Carey, Eliot Moss, Marv Solomon, and Stan Zdonik for their thoughtful and prompt feedback. We would also like to thank industry reviewers José Blakely, David Jordan, Brian Keefe, Frank Manola, and Richard Steiger for their help.

1.3.2 History

Some of the history and methodology of ODMG may be helpful in understanding our work and the philosophy behind it. We learned a lot about how to make quick progress in standards in a new industry while avoiding "design by committee."

ODMG was conceived at the invitation of the editor in the summer of 1991, in an impromptu breakfast with ODBMS vendors frustrated at the lack of progress toward ODBMS standards. Our first meeting was at SunSoft in the fall of 1991, and we released a press announcement outlining our intent in December.

The group adopted rules that have been instrumental to our quick progress. We wanted to remain small and focused. Five members turned out to be ideal — the right size for good discussion, and a small, odd number for timely voting. We admitted members as individuals, not as companies; substitute representatives from member companies would have required constant rehashing of old issues. Our membership requirements were strict: members had to devote one week per month to ODMG work, they had to be senior technical experts in the field, and their companies had to commercially ship an object database meeting the definition in this chapter. Members temporarily lost voting privileges if they missed meetings and lost their membership altogether if they repeatedly missed deliverables or meetings.

The members met quite intensely — about two days a month — to maintain our continuity and focused energy. We devised a reviewer membership to allow other important contributors to provide input without bogging down the regular meetings with many people.

Each member was responsible for a cleanly separated chapter of the overall standards document. The chair maintained a schedule and regularly hassled members in an attempt to keep deliverables on time.

In short, we were very serious about making this effort a success.

1.3.3 Next Steps

We now plan to proceed with several actions in parallel in order to keep things moving quickly:

1. Distribute this book.
2. Begin implemention of the specifications in our respective products.
3. Collect feedback and corrections for the next version of our standards specification.
4. Devise a plan for continued maintenance and development of our work by a standards group yet to be determined.
5. Submit our object model to the OMG Object Model Task Force as the ODBMS specialization of the OMG core model.
6. Submit our work to other OMG or ANSI groups, as appropriate.

If you have suggestions for improvements in future versions of our document, we welcome your input. We recommend that change proposals be submitted electronically, as follows:

1. State the essence of your proposal.
2. Outline the motivation and any pros/cons for the change.
3. State exactly what edits should be made to the text, referring to page number, section number, and paragraph.
4. Send your proposal to odmg-proposal@objects.eng.sun.com. If this email address no longer works at the time you are reading this, send your proposal to any one of the authors.

1.3.4 Contacts

To determine the latest status of the ODMG effort, please write to Morgan Kaufmann Publishers, or send electronic mail to:

odmg-info@eng.sun.com

The authors can be contacted at the following addresses:

Tom Atwood
Object Design, Inc.
1 New England Executive Park
Burlington, MA 01803
email: tom@odi.com

Rick Cattell
SunSoft, Inc.
2550 Garcia Avenue
Mountain View, CA 94043
email: rcattell@eng.sun.com

Joshua Duhl
ONTOS, Inc.
3 Burlington Woods
Burlington, MA 01803
email: duhl@ontos.com

Guy Ferran
O2 Technology
7 rue du Parc de Clagny
78000 Versailles Cedex France
email: ferran@o2tech.fr

Mary Loomis
Versant Object Technology
4500 Bohannon Drive, Suite 200
Menlo Park, CA 94025
email: mloomis@versant.com

Drew Wade
Objectivity, Inc.
800 El Camino Real
Menlo Park, CA 94025
email: drew@objy.com

1.3.5 Related Standards

There are references in this book to ANSI X3 documents, including SQL specifications (X3H2), Object Information Management (X3H7), the X3/SPARC/DBSSG OODB Task Group Report (contact fong@ecs.ncsl.nist.gov), and the C++ standard (X3J16). ANSI documents can be obtained from:

X3 Secretariat, CBEMA
1250 Eye Street, NW, Suite 200
Washington, DC 20005-3922

There are also references to Object Management Group (OMG) specifications, from the Object Request Broker (ORB) Task Force (also called CORBA), the Object Model Task Force (OMTF), and the Object Services Task Force (OSTF). OMG can be contacted at:

Object Management Group
Framingham Corporate Center
492 Old Connecticut Path
Framingham, MA 01701
email: omg@omg.org

Chapter 2

Object Model

2.1 Overview

This chapter defines the Object Model supported by ODMG-compliant implementations of object database management systems. Linear language forms for expressing schema definitions and manipulating instances of the types defined in the schema are defined in subsequent chapters of this document — a programming language-independent ODL in Chapter 3 and programming language-specific ODL/OMLs for C++ and Smalltalk in Chapters 5 and 6.

The Object Model is simply summarized:

- The basic modeling primitive is the *object*.
- Objects can be categorized into *types*. All objects of a given type exhibit common behavior and a common range of states.
- The behavior of objects is defined by a set of *operations* that can be executed on an object of the type, e.g., you can "format" an object of type Document.
- The state of objects is defined by the values they carry for a set of *properties*. These properties may be either *attributes* of the object itself or *relationships* between the object and one or more other objects.

Figure 2-1 is a sample interface definition for an object type that illustrates these basic points. An informal notation is used in this figure and for other examples in this chapter; the ODMG standard programming-language independent declaration syntax, based on OMG IDL, will be defined in Chapter 3.

```
interface Section
  {
    type properties:
        supertype: Atomic_Object;
        extent: sections;
        key: (course, section_number);

    instance properties:
        section_number: String; // unique within course
        days_offered: Set<Weekdays>;
        time_offered: Struct<from:Time, to:Time>;
        grade_curve: Set<Struct<no_of_students:Integer, grade:Integer>>;
        course: Course inverse Course::sections;
```

```
        students: Set<Student> inverse Student::take;
        taught_by: Professor inverse Professor::teaches;
        teaching_assistants: Set<TA> inverse TA::responsible_for;

    instance operations:
        cancel ();
        reschedule(from: Struct<date: Date, time: Time>,
                to: Struct<date: Date, time: Time> ) raises (unavailable);
        post_grades ();
};
```

Figure 2-1. A Sample Object Type Definition

A type has one *interface* and one or more *implementations*. The interface defines the external interface supported by instances of the type — that is, their properties and the operations that can be invoked on them. An implementation, by contrast, defines *data structures* in terms of which instances of the type are physically represented and the *methods* that operate on those data structures to support the externally visible state and behavior defined in the interface.

Types are themselves objects, and may therefore have properties themselves. The interface definition of a type specifies *values* for these *type properties*. Two type properties are illustrated in the example — the *supertypes* of an object type, the *extent* of an object type, and the *keys* of an object type.

- *Supertypes*. Object types are related in a subtype/supertype graph, e.g., Associate_Professor is a subtype of Professor; Professor is a subtype of Person. All of the attributes, relationships, and operations defined on a supertype are inherited by the subtype. The subtype may add additional properties and operations to introduce behavior or state unique to instances of the subtype. It may also "refine" the properties and operations it inherits to specialize them to the behavior and range of state values appropriate for instances of the subtype.
- *Extents*. The set of all instances of a given type is termed its *extent*. The type programmer can request that the system automatically maintain a current index to the members of this set by including an extent declaration in the type definition. The maintenance of the extent is optional and need not be done for all types.
- *Keys*. In some cases the individual instances of a type can be uniquely identified by the value they carry for some property or set of properties. These properties or sets of properties are termed *keys*. *Simple keys* are keys that consist of a single property. *Compound keys* consist of a set of properties. Note that relationships as well as attributes may serve as keys or part of keys. In Figure 2-1, sections are numbered within courses. The compound

key that uniquely identifies a section is therefore a (course, section_number) pair.

If you will refer to Figure 2-1 again, you will note that the interface definition for an object type also contains instance property and instance operation declarations. Instance properties are the properties for which objects of the type carry values. Instance operations are the operations which objects of the type support. Some additional details regarding these declarations that can be seen in the sample interface definition include the following:

- The operations that objects of a given type support are specified as a set of *operation signatures*. Each signature defines the name of the operation, the name and type of any arguments, the name and type of any returned values, and the names of any *exceptions* (error conditions) the operation can raise.
- The attributes for which objects of a given type carry values are specified as a set of *attribute signatures*. Each signature defines the name of the attribute and the type of its legal values. Attributes take *literals* as values, e.g., strings, numbers, etc.
- The relationships in which objects of a given type participate are specified as a set of *relationship signatures*. Each signature defines the type of the other object or set of objects involved in the relationship and the name of a *traversal function* used to refer to the related object or set of objects. Relationships are binary and are defined between two objects (as opposed to attributes that are defined between an object and a literal). The cardinality of the relationship can be one-to-one, one-to-many, and many-to-many. In Figure 2-1 course is a one-to-one relationship between a section and the course of which it is an offering; teaching_assistants is a one-to-many relationship between a section and the TAs assigned to teach this section of the course.
- The model includes a built-in set of collection types — sets, bags, lists, arrays, and so on. Named instances of these types can be used to group objects, e.g., honors_candidates might group the set of students whose grade_point_average is over 90.

The major types built into the object model are shown in Figure 2-2 below. In the figure, indentation has been used to show subtype/supertype relationships between types. The type Attribute, for instance, is a subtype of the type Property.

- ❑ Denotable_Object
  - ❑ Object
  - ❑ Literal
- ❑ Characteristic
  - ❑ Operation
  - ❑ Property
    - ❑ Attribute
    - ❑ Relationship

Figure 2-2. Basic Type Hierarchy of the Object Model

Sections 2.2 through 2.7 of this chapter explain the model by walking through the type hierarchy in roughly top-down order. Section 2.8 summarizes the full type hierarchy and discusses the metatype structure that supports it. Section 2.9 discusses transactions. Section 2.10 discusses operations on the database as a whole. Section 2.11 outlines the principal functionality under consideration for inclusion in a future version of the object model.

2.2 Types and Instances

A type defines the state and behavior of its instances. As we will see below, state is defined as a set of *properties;* behavior is defined as a set of *operations* (Sections 2.4 and 2.5). When we don't need to distinguish between the state and behavior of a type we will refer to its *characteristics.*

The set of all instances of a type is called the *extent* of the type.

2.2.1 Inheritance

Types may be organized into a graph of subtypes and supertypes. A subtype inherits all of the characteristics of its supertypes. It may also define additional characteristics that apply only to its instances. The intention is that an instance of a subtype may be treated like an instance of each of its supertypes. An instance of the subtype supports all of the state and behavior of the supertype as well as new state and/or behavior unique to its more specialized nature.

Some types are directly instantiable. Others are termed *abstract types.* Abstract types only define characteristics inherited by their subtypes. They do not define an implementation and therefore cannot be directly instantiated. An instantiable subtype of an abstract type must define an implementation that supports each of the characteristics inherited from its abstract supertypes.

Although the built-in types at the root of the object model have been organized as a tree, the graph of user-defined types in a database schema may in general be a directed acyclic graph. This raises the possibility that a type will inherit characteristics that have the same name (but different semantics) from two different supertypes. This form of name clash is handled by requiring the inheriting type to redefine the name of one of the inherited characteristics. For example, if type D was defined as a subtype of types B and C, and both type B and type C defined an operation expand, then type D would have to include a specification such as become_larger redefines B.expand.

Note that within the type graph that defines the built-in types of the ODMG Object Model (Figure 2-2), inheritance is used within the subtree below Characteristic just as it is within the subtree below Denotable_Object. In the base level of the ODMG model, the application builder may only define subtypes within the tree below type Object. Neither the abstract types Characteristic or Property, nor the types Attribute or Relationship may be subtyped. This is a restriction that we anticipate will be relaxed in a future version of the ODMG Object Model.

2.2.2 Extents

The *extent* of a type is the set of all instances of the type. By calling out the extent as a declaration in the object type definition, the type definer instructs the ODBMS to automatically maintain the extent of the type as instances of this type are created and deleted.

There is a direct correspondence between the intentional notion *type* and the extensional notion *extent*. If an object is an *instance* of the type A, then it will of necessity be a *member* of the extent of A. Similarly, if type A is a *subtype* of type B, then the extent of A will be a *subset* of the extent of B.

2.2.3 Implementations and Classes

A type has one or more *implementations*. In the base model it is only object types (not property or operation types) that have a user-definable implementation. An implementation of an object type consists of a *representation* and a set of *methods*. The representation is a set of data structures. The methods are procedure bodies. There is one method for each of the operations defined in the specification. These methods implement the behavior specified for their associated operation by modifying the representation of the object and/or invoking operations defined on related objects. There may be additional methods and data structures in the implementation that have no counterpart operations in the type interface.

Implementations are named. Names of implementations are unique within the scope defined by a type. The implementation(s) associated with a type are lexically separate in ODL.

The combination of the type interface specification and one of the implementations defined for the type is termed a *class*. This use of the term "class" makes a subset of the ODMG model roughly consonant with the C++ model. A C++ class has a single *public part* and a single *private part*. The private part corresponds to the implementation in ODL. The ODMG model is richer than the C++ model in that it allows multiple implementations for a given interface. From the ODBMS implementor's viewpoint, this is useful to support databases that span networks that include machines with different architectures, and to support mixed-language or mixed-compiler environments. From the programmer's viewpoint, it is useful because it allows the programmer to define different implementations of a type to meet different performance versus space versus recoverability trade-offs. In the absence of multiple implementations for a single type, the type programmer would be forced to abuse the subtype mechanism to achieve this differentiation — defining a distinct subtype for each distinct implementation of a type. Set_as_Btree and Set_as_Linked_List would be introduced, for example, as subtypes of the type Set, rather than as alternate implementations for the type Set.

Which implementation an object uses is specified at object creation time. The base model provides no facilities for dynamically changing the implementation of an object later.

2.3 Objects

Objects are the things of which characteristics are predicated. Stated less formally, objects have state and behavior.

Objects also have identity. Individual objects have an intrinsic identity in and of themselves. This is in contrast to instances of characteristic types that can only be identified by picking out the objects to which the characteristics apply.

2.3.1 Type Denotable_Object

The hierarchy of object types is rooted at the type Denotable_Object. There are two orthogonal lines along which the set of denotable objects can be decomposed— (1) mutable versus immutable, and (2) atomic versus structured. Instead of representing this as a lattice within the built-in type hierarchy of the Object Model, we have chosen to flatten the lattice into a hierarchy by taking mutable/immutable as the first distinction, and then repeating the atomic/structured distinction under both the mutable and immutable branches of the tree. The mutable/immutable distinction is captured within the type hierarchy using the more traditional terms Object and Literal. Objects are mutable; literals are immutable. The result is a base hierarchy as follows:

- ❑ Denotable Object
- ❑ Object
    - ❑ Atomic_Object
    - ❑ Structured_Object
- ❑ Literal
    - ❑ Atomic_Literal
    - ❑ Structured_Literal

All denotable objects have identity, but the representation used to maintain that identity is typically different for objects and literals. The representation of the identity of a literal is typically the bit pattern that encodes its value. The representation of the identity of an object is what we refer to as an *object identifier* (often abbreviated *OID*) — a unique bit pattern generated solely for the purpose of uniquely identifying a particular object. Both objects and literals inherit the equal? operation from type Denotable_Object. However, they are not constrained to use the same representation for the identifiers that allow them to execute that operation.

2.3.2 Type Object

Instances of type Object are mutable. The values of their attributes may change. The relationships in which they participate may change. But the identity of the object remains invariant across these changes.

2.3.2.1 Object Identity

An object's identity uniquely distinguishes the object from all other objects within the *domain* in which the object was created. This identity is referred to as an *object identifier*, as just discussed. In the base model the domain of an object identifier is the database in which the object exists. The structure of the bit pattern representing an object identifier is not defined by the Object Model; this is considered a representation issue. The operations defined in the model are independent of the representation of object identifiers.

Changing the values of the attributes of an object, or the relationships in which it participates, does not change the identity of the object. It remains the same object.

2.3.2.2 Object Names

Individual objects may be given names meaningful to the programmer or end-user in addition to object identifiers. Any object will have a single object identifier, but it may have more than one name. However, a name must refer uniquely to a single object within the scope of the definition of the name. From the vantage point of a program written to use the database, the database adds a new outermost scope to those defined within the program. In the base level model this scope defines a single flat name space across the entire database. There is no notion of a hierarchy or lattice of name spaces within the database, or of name spaces that span databases.

Given a persistent object, it is possible to determine at runtime whether the object has a name and, if so, what that name is. If an object has multiple names within a given name scope, it is possible to determine at runtime all of these names.

2.3.2.3 Object Descriptions

Objects may also be identified by *predicates* defined on their characteristics. A predicate is applied to a collection to select the members of the collection that satisfy the predicate. (See the select and select_one operations defined on type Collection in Section 2.6, below.) A predicate is a boolean conjunction or disjunction of operations supported by the object types that appear within the predicate.

A common simple case of this is selecting an object that has a particular value for one of its properties from the extent of a type. To accelerate the processing of such associative selection requests (commonly called "queries"), a type definer may declare that the values of certain properties are sufficient to uniquely identify objects within the extent of their associated type. Such a declaration implicitly requests the ODBMS to automatically create and maintain indices on the properties or combinations of properties that uniquely identify particular objects.

2.3.2.4 Inheritance among subtypes of type *Object*

An object type may be defined as a subtype of one or more other object types, e.g.,

```
interface Associate_Professor: Professor { ... }
```

If object type B is declared to be a subtype of object type A, this means that any operations defined on A are also available on instances of B, any attributes defined on A are also defined on B, and any relationships defined on A are also available on instances of B.

The model requires only type inheritance; it neither mandates nor precludes separate treatment of implementation inheritance.

2.3.2.5 Properties of Objects

The following built-in properties are defined on type Object:

- has_name?: Boolean
- names: Set<String>
- type: Type

2.3.2.6 Operations on Objects

The following built-in operations are defined on type Object:

- delete()
- same_as? (oid: Object_id) —> b: Boolean

A brief comment on the notation used in this chapter for operation signatures. Operation signatures are shown in the form:

```
operation_name ([argument{,argument}])[ —> result]
```

where:

{ symbol } means a sequence of 0 or o symbol(s)
[symbol] means an optional symbol

and where

argument ::= argument_name: argument_type, and
result ::= result_name: Result_type

The simplest form of operation signature is therefore just operation_name(). But an operation may have one or more arguments, and may return an object as a result. The type of the object returned is Result_type. Arguments shown in braces are optional.

The create operation allocates storage for the representation of the object, assigns an Object_id, and returns that id as the value of the operation. The programmer may optionally provide a set of (property_name, property_value) pairs as arguments to the create operation. These values will be used to initialize the corresponding properties of the object at the time it is created. An attempt to retrieve the value of a property that has not been initialized or assigned a value prior to the time the retrieval operation is executed will return nil as the value of the property.

The delete operation removes the object from the database and frees the storage used by its representation. Deleting an object removes it from any relationships in which it participated. A subsequent attempt to 'reach' it by traversing such a relationship will raise an exception. Deleting an object does not recursively delete other objects related to the deleted object. If the object is an instance of a type for which an extent is being maintained by the ODBMS, deleting the object will remove the object from the extent of the type of which it was an instance. The Object_id of a deleted object is not reused.

The two forms of the same_as operation return the boolean true if both of their arguments refer to the same object, and false otherwise.

2.3.2.7 Object Lifetime

The lifetime of a mutable object is orthogonal to its type. Three lifetimes are supported in the base model:

- coterminus_with_procedure;
- coterminus_with_process;
- coterminus_with_database.

An object whose lifetime is coterminus_with_procedure is typically one declared in the heading of a procedure. Its storage is allocated out of the stack frame created by the programming language runtime when the procedure is invoked, and is returned to the free pool when the procedure returns. An object of lifetime coterminus_with_process is typically allocated by the programming language runtime out of either static storage or the heap. An object of lifetime coterminus_with_database is typically allocated out of a storage segment, page, cluster, or heap managed by the ODBMS runtime. Specific programming languages may introduce other lifetimes consistent with their block structure.

In the base model the lifetime of an object is specified at the time the object is created and cannot be changed thereafter. Objects of longer lifetimes can validly refer to objects of shorter lifetimes only for the period of time during which the shorter lifetime object is known to exist.

2.3.3 Literals (immutable objects)

Literals are objects whose instances are immutable. Two subtypes of literal are defined by the model — atomic literals and structured literals. Numbers and characters are examples of atomic literals. There is no explicit create operation defined on atomic literals; all instances of atomic literal types implicitly pre-exist. Instances of atomic literal types have unique identity, but do not have OIDs. The model supports the following subtypes of the type Atomic_Literal:

- Integer
- Float
- Boolean
- Character

The precision of the arithmetic types and the size of the Character type is left open to the specific language bindings. The intent of the model is that a programming language binding should support the language-specific analog of these types, as well as any subtypes defined by the programming language, e.g., long_int, double, . . . in C++. If the programming language does not contain an analog for one of the types defined by the model, then a class library defining the type should be supplied as part of the programming language binding.

The type Structured_Literal has two subtypes — Immutable_Collection and Immutable_Structure. These types are the direct analogues of their counterpart Structured_Object types, Structure and Collection, except that they are immutable. For an attribute that takes a structured literal as its value, it is possible to replace the value of the attribute with a new structured literal, but it is not possible to update the original structured literal. The built-in subtypes of Immutable_Collection and Immutable_Structure are the following:

- Immutable_Collection
  - Bit_String
  - Character_String
  - Enumeration
- Immutable_Structure
  - Date
  - Time
  - DateTime
  - Interval

The types Date, Time, DateTime, and Interval are defined as in the ANSI SQL specification.

Enumeration is a type generator. Each enumeration declaration occurring within an object type declaration defines an unnamed type that has only the instances named in the enumeration declaration. These instances have only names; they have no properties and no operations. The representation of the types generated by an enumeration declaration is left open to the specific language bindings.

The type programmer may define additional subtypes of type Literal. He may not, however, redefine operations defined on any of the built-in literal types. This is an implementation restriction imposed because the operations defined on many literals are implemented directly in the hardware or firmware of the machines on which the ODBMS runs.

2.4 Modeling State — Properties

An object type defines a set of *properties* through which users of instances of the type can interrogate and in some cases directly manipulate the state of these instances. Two kinds of property are defined in the model — *attribute* and *relationship*. Attributes are defined on one object type and take literals as their values. Relationships are defined between two object types, both mutable (nonliteral) object types. Although there are relationships between literals implicit in the algebra of the built-in operations on types such as Integer (e.g., 3>5), the programmer using the ODBMS may define relationships only between mutable (nonliteral) object types. For example the grade_point_average attribute defined on objects of type Student takes as its value an integer; integers are literals. The advisor/advisee relationship is defined between two object types — Student and Professor. Sections 2.4.1 and 2.4.2 below discuss attributes and relationships in greater detail.

2.4.1 Attributes

Attributes are defined on a single object type. The declaration of an object type includes declarations of each of the attribute types for which an instance of the object type carries a specific value. Attributes do not have OIDs. Their individuality is determined by the individual object to which they apply. For example, the object type Person might contain the attribute type definitions:

age: Integer
sex: Enumeration (male, female)
height: Integer

A particular instance of the type Person, say John, might have the corresponding attribute instances: John.age=32, John.sex=male, and John.height=72.

An attribute takes as its value a literal or a set of literals (actually any structured type containing only literals). See Section 2.3.3 above for a list of the built-in literal types, and Section 2.6 below for a list of the built-in aggregate types.

The following built-in operations are defined on attributes:

set_value (new_value: Literal)
get_value () —> existing_value: Literal

The algebra of these operations (what they do and how they interact) is as follows.

The set_value operation gives the attribute a new value, replacing whatever value it currently has (including nil). The next get_value operation will return the literal supplied as the argument to the set_value.

The get_value operation returns the current value of the attribute, i.e., the value set by the most immediately preceding set_value call, unless no set_value call has been issued against this attribute. In that case it returns the default value if one was specified in the lexically containing object type definition, or if not, the distinguished value nil.

The model allows the type definer to specify an initial value, and provides a distinguished nil value. Functionality equivalent to a clear_value operation is provided by set_value(nil).

Attributes define abstract state. They therefore appear within the interface definition of an object type rather than in the implementation. There is no implication that an attribute is implemented as a field in a data structure. The get_value operation on the age attribute defined on type Person, for instance, might be implemented as a method that derives the person's age from his date_of_birth and the current date, rather than storing it in some data structure used to represent instances of type Person.

In the base model, attributes are not "first class." It is not possible to define attributes of attributes, to define relationships between attributes, or to add subtype specific operations to attributes. It is possible to override the built-in get_value and set_value operations of particular attribute types. This allows the type definer to provide trigger functionality on the getting or setting of an attribute value, and to do arbitrarily complex constraint evaluation on their invocation, e.g., for a set_value operation.

Note that an implementation may allow the programmer to call the above-specified operations directly, or it may provide a simpler surface syntax consistent with that of the programming language through which the programmer is accessing the objects. An implementation might, for instance, allow the type definer to specify an initial value as part of the object type declaration, e.g., age: Integer default 12. A preprocessor or compiler would turn this declaration into a call to the set_value operation passing the literal "12" as an argument. This call would be inserted into the constructor for objects of the type on which age was defined. Similarly, a preprocessor or compiler would allow the programmer to use normal assignment statement syntax, e.g., obj.att = <literal>, uniformly for all attributes — those that had overridden the

get_value and **set_value** calls as well as those that had not. For those that had overridden the **get_value** and **set_value** calls, the generated code would explicitly invoke the refinements of the built-in routines supplied by the type definer. For those that had not overridden the **get_value** and **set_value** operations, the generated code would typically be an in-line expansion of the body of the relevant operation. This would allow an ODBMS implementation to offer the type definer the flexibility of supplying type-specific **get_value** and **set_value** operations without sacrificing the performance of in-line code for dereferencing objects.

2.4.2 Relationships

Relationship types are defined between (mutable) object types. The base Object Model supports only binary relationships, not n-ary relationships. One-to-one, one-to-many, and many-to-many relationships are supported.

Relationships themselves have no names. Instead, named *traversal paths* are defined for each direction of traversal, e.g., a student *takes* a set of courses; conversely, a course *is_taken_by* a set of students. These names are declared within the interface definitions of the object types that participate in the relationship. In the university example the **takes** traversal path would be defined within the interface declaration for the **Student** object type. The **is_taken_by** traversal path would be declared within the interface definition for the **Course** object type. The fact that these traversal paths both apply to the same relationship type is indicated by an *inverse* clause in both of the traversal path declarations, e.g.:

```
interface Student
    { ...
        takes: Set<Course> inverse Course::is_taken_by
    }
```

and

```
interface Course
    { ...
        is_taken_by: Set<Student> inverse Student::takes
    )
```

If the type programmer does not specify an inverse path for a relationship, only one direction of traversal will be possible and an ODBMS may take this as a hint to use an implementation of the relationship type that does not carry the overhead of the pointer or other mechanism used to support traversal in the opposite direction.

Relationships maintain referential integrity. If an object that participates in a relationship is deleted, a subsequent attempt to traverse the relationship (in either direction) will raise an exception.

Relationship instances do not have OIDs. They are uniquely identified by the object instances that participate in them.

One-to-many relationships may be ordered. Many-to-many relationships may be ordered in either or both directions of traversal.

There is a single instance of any many-to-many relationship type. That instance in turn implies the existance of two sets of one-to-many relationships. And each of these relationships in turn implies the existance of a set of one-to-one relationships.

The operations defined on a many-to-many relationship are the following:

- delete()
- add_one_to_one (o1: Denotable_Object, o2: Denotable_Object)
- remove_one_to_one (o1: Denotable_Object, o2: Denotable_Object)
- add_one_to_many (o1: Denotable_Object, s: Set<Denotable_Object>)
- remove_one_to_many (o1: Denotable_Object, s: Set<Denotable_Object>)
- remove_all_from (o1: Denotable_Object)

The operations defined on a one_to_many relationship are the following:

- create (o1: Denotable_Object, s: Set<Denotable_Object>)
- delete()
- add_one_to_one (o1: Denotable_Object, o2: Denotable_Object)
- remove_one_to_one (o1: Denotable_Object, o2: Denotable_Object)
- traverse(from: Denotable_Object) —> s: Set<Denotable_Object>

The operations defined on a one-to-one relationship are the following:

- create (o1:Denotable_Object, o2:Denotable_Object)
- delete()
- traverse (from:Denotable_Object) —> to:Denotable_Object

Note that there is no traverse operation defined on many-to-many relationships. One uses the traverse operations defined on the component one-to-many relationships. Note also that there is only a traverse function defined for one direction of traversal of a one-to-many relationship, i.e., from the single object to the set of related objects. There is, however, a traverse operation defined on each of the component one-to-one relationships that allows one to go from any element of the set to the single related object.

2.5 Modeling Behavior — Operations

The potential behavior of instances of an object type is specified as a set of *operations*.

For each operation, an *operation signature* is included in the object type definition by the type programmer. The signature includes the argument names and types, exceptions potentially raised, and types of the values returned, if any. Operations are always defined on a single object type. There is no notion of an operation independent of an object type, or of an operation defined on two or more object types.

Operation names need be unique only within a single type definition. This leaves open the possibility that operations defined on different types will have the same name. These are called *overloaded operations*. When an operation is invoked using an overloaded name, a specific operation is selected for execution. This selection, sometimes called *operation name resolution* and sometimes *operation dispatching*, is based on the type of the object supplied as the first argument of the actual call. Given that object types can be ordered into a hierarchy, the object supplied as the first argument on a call might have several types. The operation defined on the most specific type of the argument object is chosen for invocation.

An argument can be any denotable object — mutable or literal, structured or atomic.

An operation may return a denotable object or a set of such objects. There is a distinguished denotable object returned which is treated as the value of the operation itself to allow functional composition of operations. For an operation that has only side effects, the returned value is nil.

An operation may have side effects. The model does not distinguish a subcategory of operation that is side-effect-free. The programmer might, however, want to distinguish such operations in a pragma — especially those that occurred within query expressions. In the absence of such a pragma, the query optimizer will be forced to take a very conservative strategy in generating code to evaluate queries containing references to operations on user-defined types.

There is no formal specification of the semantics of an operation, although it is good practice to include a comment that specifies the purpose of the operation, any side effects it has, pre and post conditions, and any invariants it is intended to preserve.

The built-in operations defined on type Operation are the following:

- invoke()
- return()
- return_abnormally (e: Exception)

For most compiled languages, these operations cannot be explicitly invoked by the programmer. The occurrence of an operation name within a statement of the programming language is instead compiled by the compiler into the code which invokes the named operation. It is instructive to think of this as open-coding the invoke operation.

The model assumes sequential execution of operations. It does not require support for concurrent or parallel operations. However, it does not preclude an ODBMS from providing such support.

The model does not require support for remote operations. However, it does not preclude an ODBMS from providing such support. The default site of execution of an operation is the site at which it was invoked. An ODBMS may define pragmas that allow the programmer to specify a preferred site of execution on each operation invocation, or policies that determine a default location other than the site of execution.

2.5.1 Exception Model

The object model supports dynamically nested exception handlers, using a termination model of exception handling. Exceptions are themselves objects and may be organized into a subtype/supertype hierarchy. A root type Exception is provided by the ODBMS. This type includes an operation to print out a message noting that an unhandled exception of type <exception_type> has occurred and to terminate the process. Information on the cause of an exception or the context in which it occurred is passed back to the exception handler as properties of the exception object.

Control flow is as follows:

- The programmer declares an exception handler within scope <s> capable of handling exceptions of type <t>.
- An operation within a contained scope <sn> may "raise" an exception of type <t>.
- The exception is "caught" by the most immediately containing scope that has an exception handler. The call stack is automatically unwound by the runtime out to the level of the handler. Destructors are called for all objects allocated in intervening stack frames. Any transactions begun within a nested scope that is unwound by the runtime in the process of searching down the stack for an exception handler are aborted.
- When control reaches the handler, the handler may either decide that it can handle the exception or pass it on (reraise it) to a containing handler.
- Once an exception has been handled, control resumes at the statement following the call to the operation that causes the exception.

An exception handler that declares itself capable of handling exceptions of type <t>, will also handle exceptions of any subtype of <t>. A programmer who requires more specific control over exceptions of a specific subtype of <t> may declare a handler for this more specific subtype within a contained scope.

The signature for an operation includes a declaration of the exceptions that the operation can raise.

2.6 Structured Objects

The type Structured_Object has two subtypes — Structure and Collection.

Structures have a fixed number of named slots each of which contains an object or a literal. The types of the elements that fill the slots may be (and usually are) different.

Insertion of objects into slots of the structure and removal of objects from slots in the structure are both done by referring to these named slots, e.g., address.zip_code = 01907.

Collections, by contrast, contain an arbitrary number of elements, do not have named slots, and contain elements that are all instances of the same type. It is possible to have elements that are instances of different subtypes of the type over which the collection was defined, but this does not constitute an exception to the rule, since an object that is an instance of type T_1 is also an instance of type T_2 if T_2 is the supertype of T_1. Insertion of elements is based on either absolute position within the collection (at the beginning/end) or at a point established by a cursor (before/after the current element). Retrieval is based on either absolute position, current cursor-relative position, or a predicate that uniquely selects an element from the collection based on the value(s) that object carries for one or more of its properties.

Within collections, the model supports both ordered and unordered collections, where the order is defined either by the sequence in which objects are inserted or by the value of one of the properties of the objects that are the members of the collection. Collections may also allow or disallow the same object to be present in the collection more than once.

The result is a substructure below Structured_Object as follows:

- ❑ Structured_Object
  - ❑ Collection
    - ❑ Set
    - ❑ Bag
    - ❑ List
    - ❑ Array
  - ❑ Structure

Structured objects may be freely composed. The model supports sets of structures, structures of sets, arrays of structures, etc. This allows the definition of types like Dictionary as an ordered set whose elements are structures containing two fields: a key and an object identifier. Indexing is done on the key field. The select_one() operation returns the element that matches the key supplied as an argument to the operation.

The Object Model defines both mutable and immutable collections. Mutable collections carry an intensional semantics; immutable collections carry an extensional semantics. Mutable collections are defined as subtypes of Structured_Object. Immutable collections are defined as subtypes of Structured_Literal (see Section 2.7). The subtree of structured types below Structured_Object includes Collection, Set, Bag, List, Array, and Structure. Instances of these types are all mutable. That is to say, a collection or structure retains its identity even if its members change. As an example, the set my_favorite_books remains the same set even if a new book is added to the set. This is in contrast to the extensional treatment of sets in the simpler forms of mathematical logic. In an extensional treatment, two sets are the same if and only if they have the same members. This means that a member cannot be added to or removed from a set; the only operation is to create a new set. It is also the case that two sets are the same set if they have the same members, regardless of the intention implied by their name. The classical example of this in the literature of mathematical logic is the set of unicorns and the set of living_kings_of_France. If both of these sets have the same members (i.e., none) then they are, in the extentional treatment, the same set. This does not seem to be the way most people treat sets in their everyday world. The ODMG Object Model therefore treats the intentional model as the "unmarked" case. The type Set is mutable; its immutable analogue is explicitly identified as an Immutable_Set.

2.6.1 Collections

A collection is an object that groups other objects. Examples are a set of students, and a list of classes. All of the elements of a collection must be of the same type.

Collections may be defined over any instantiable subtype of type Denotable_Object. Collections of atomic objects, atomic literals, collections of collections, collections of structures, etc., are all legal.

Note that in an implementation binding the object model to programming languages that allow the programmer to directly manipulate references to objects or addresses of objects, collections may be defined over references to objects and/or pointers to objects.

Individual collections are instances of collection types. Collection types are instantiations of collection *type generators*. Collection type generators are also called *parameterized types*. The type generator for List<T>, for example, would be defined as:

```
parameterized type List <T>
  {
      T element
      ...
  }
```

The type List <T> can be instantiated to produce the type List<Course> by supplying it with the element type Course as an argument.

Parameterized types allow type checking to be performed at compile time rather than at runtime. An attempt to insert or remove an object whose type is not compatible with that of the collection's element type will cause the compiler to flag the offending statement as an error.

Each collection has an immutable identity, just like any other object. Two collections may have the same elements without being therefore the same collection. Similarly, inserting, removing, or modifying an element of a collection does not create a new collection. The collection remains the same collection. There are two subtypes of collection: *predicate_defined* and *insertion_defined.* The only predicate_defined collections in the base model are extents. All other collections must be explicitly maintained by the application writer. Creating an object that satisfies the predicate that defines a collection will not automatically cause that object to be inserted into the collection. Nor will modifying an object so that it no longer satisfies the predicate that defines a collection automatically cause the object to be removed from the collection. However, the fact that collections must be explicitly maintained by the application programmer does not change their intended semantics — anything that meets the predicate should go in the collection. Extents are predicate-defined collections where the predicate is "Is of type <T>" where <T> is the type whose instances are the members of the extent.

2.6.2 Iteration over Collections

It is possible to iterate over the elements of a collection. Iteration is done by defining an iterator that maintains a current position within the collection to be traversed. The first, last, and next operations defined on type Iterator establish/move the current position and return the element at that position. For unordered collections the order of iteration is arbitrary. For ordered collections it can be either first to last or last to first.

```
type Iterator<T>
   properties:
      stable?: Boolean
      iteration_order: Enumeration (forward, backward)
   operations:
      next() —> element: T
      first() —> element: T
      last() —> element: T
      more?()—>b: Boolean
      reset ()
      delete ()
```

The next operation positions the iterator at the collection's next element and returns that element. If there is no next element, next returns nil. After next is applied to the last element of the collection, the value of the iterator becomes nil. The initial call to next returns the first element of the collection if the iteration_order is forward and the last element if the iteration_order is backward. The next operations return nil rather than raising an exception to simplify programming loops that iterate through the elements of a collection.

The more? operation returns boolean true when the iterator is still positioned at some element of the collection, and boolean false when the iterator is nil.

Iterator<T> is a type generator. The parameter T is the element type of the collection to be traversed.

There is no create operation defined on type Iterator. Instead there is a create_iterator operation defined on type Collection. There may be more than one iterator defined on a given collection.

2.6.2.1 Updates During Iteration

It is possible to define queries in which the collection is updated while the program is traversing its elements, for example:

```
all_components: Bag<Part>;
widget: Part;
p: Part;
all_components := widget;
foreach p in all_components do {
   all_components := all_components union p.components
   };
```

For unordered collections, the semantics of insertion into collections and update of a member of a collection are defined so that the above code fragment will always work. Queries over ordered collections, however, will still work only if an element inserted during an iteration is inserted later, in the order of iteration, than the position of the iterator within the collection at the time of insertion.

2.6.3 Built-in Collection Subtypes

The object model defines a standard set of built-in collection type generators:

- Set <T>
- Bag <T>
- List <T>
- Array <T>

These are all subtypes of the type generator Collection <T>. The attributes and operations defined on the types that each of the built-in type generators generate are specified in the subsections that follow.

2.6.3.1 Collection<T>

The type Collection<T> cannot be directly instantiated. It is an abstract type only. It defines the following properties and supports the following operations:

properties:

- cardinality: Integer
- empty?: Boolean

- ordered?: Boolean
- allows_duplicates?: Boolean

operations:

- create ([pragma {, pragma}]) —> c:Collection<T>
  where pragma ::= clustering | expected_cardinality | representation
- delete ()
- copy (c2: Collection<T>[pragma {, pragma}])
  where pragma ::= clustering | representation
- insert_element (o: Denotable_Object)
- remove_element (o: Denotable_Object)
- remove_element_at (current_position: Iterator)
- replace_element_at (o: Denotable_Object, current_position: Iterator)
- retrieve_element_at (current_position: Iterator) —>element: T
- select_element (predicate: String) —> element:T
- select (predicate: String) —> c: Collection<T>
- exists? (predicate: String) —> b: Boolean
- contains_element? (o: Denotable_Object) —> b: Boolean
- create_iterator(stable: Boolean) —>i: Iterator

Note that in a programming language implementation that makes references to objects and/or addresses of objects visible to the programmer, the create, copy, and select operations may be defined to return a reference to a set rather than the set itself.

Implementations may also define the following storage and performance related properties and operations on type Collection. Support for these operations is optional, however, as are all pragma-related characteristics.

properties:

- indexed?:Boolean

operations:

- create_index (on: property of element [,t: Index_type])
- create_index (on: component of element [t: Index_type])
- create_index (on: function [, t: Index_type])
- create_index (on: value [,t: Index_type])
- drop_index ()

The create_index operation allows the programmer to specifically request creation of an index on the elements of a collection. If the collection is a collection of atomic objects, the index may be on any property defined by the type of the objects. If the collection is a collection of structured objects, the index may be on any component of the structured object. If the collection is a collection of atomic literals, the index may be defined on the value of the literal. If the collection is a collection of structured literals, the index may be defined on some component of the structured literal. Indices may also be defined on the results of a programmer-supplied function that is applied at index creation time to each member of the collection. The second argument allows the programmer to specify the type of index to be created. Typical index types include B-trees, L-trees, and hash-tables.

The create operation may take additional, implementation-specific arguments that serve as pragmas specifying where a collection is to be created, how it is to be clustered, expected cardinality, and expected access pattern.

The copy operation replaces the contents of collection c2 with those of the collection on which the operation is invoked.

The cursor-based functions remove_element_at, replace_element_at, and retrieve_element_at can be used on all collections, ordered or unordered.

The select operation takes as its argument a string containing a predicate. The predicate is applied to each element of the collection. Those that satisfy the predicate are returned as members of the resulting subcollection. By default, the subcollection returned is of the same type as that being queried, i.e., if the query is executed against a set, the subcollection returned is a set; if the query is executed against a list, the subcollection returned will be a list; if the query is executed against a bag, the subcollection returned will be a bag; if the query is executed against a variable length array, the subcollection returned will be a variable length array of the size necessary to hold the result. Note that since the collection types defined by the base model are intentional types, this implies that the result of a query will also be an intentional collection. A predicate is, in general, a boolean conjunction or disjunction of expressions. For embedded query sublanguages within traditional programming languages, these are expressions of the base programming language or of the query sublanguage. For stand-alone query languages, these are expressions as defined by the stand-alone query language. Queries may be run over any collection — system-maintained collections like extents or programmer-maintained collections. The ODBMS will specify a protocol that a collection implementation has to support in order for queries to work.

2.6.3.2 Type Set<T>

Sets are unordered collections that do not allow duplicates.

Set<T> refines the following operations inherited from type Collection<T>:

- create ()—> s: Set<T>
- insert_element (o: T)

Set<T> defines the following operations:

- union (s2: Set<T>) —> s3: Set<T>
- intersection (s2: Set<T>) —> s3: Set<T>
- difference (s2: Set<T>) —> s3: Set<T>
- copy (s2: Set<T>) —> s2: Set<T>

- is_subset? (s2: Set<T>) —> b: Boolean
- is_proper_subset? (s2: Set<T>) —> b: Boolean
- is superset? (s2: Set<T>) —> b: Boolean
- is_proper_superset? (s2: Set<T>) —> b: Boolean

The create operation creates a new set whose elements are restricted to being objects of type T or of a subtype of type T.

The insert_element operation inserts the object passed as its argument into an existing set. If the object passed as an argument is already a member of the set, the operation does nothing. It does not raise an exception.

The union operation returns a new set whose elements are the union of the elements of the two original sets.

The intersection operation returns a new set whose elements are the intersection of the elements of the original sets.

The difference operation returns a new set whose elements are the set theoretic difference between the elements of the original set and that passed as an argument to the difference operation.

The copy operation returns a new set whose elements are the same as the elements of the original set. It is a shallow copy operation. It does not copy the objects that were members of the original set, nor does it copy objects referred to by these objects.

2.6.3.3 Type Bag <T>

Bags are unordered collections that allow duplicates.

Bag<T> refines the following operations inherited from type Collection<T>:

- create () —> b: Bag<T>
- insert_element (o: T)
- remove_element (element: T)
- select (predicate: String) —> b: Bag<T>

Bag<T> defines the following operations:

- union (b2: Bag<T>) —> b3: Bag<T>
- intersection (b2: Bag<T>) —> b3: Bag<T>
- difference (b2: Bag<T>) —> b3: Bag<T>

The create operation returns a collection of type Bag<T>.

The insert_element operation inserts the denotable object passed as an argument into the collection. If the object is already a member of the bag, it is inserted a second time.

The remove_element operation reduces the count of the object within the collection by one.

The behavior of the set-theoretic operators can be understood in terms of performing an iteration on one or more of the operands. Assignment of one bag to another through- bag_1.copy(bag_2) is equivalent to first removing all of bag_2's elements, and then performing an insert into bag_1 for each occurrence of each element of bag_2. The union() operator — bag_1.union (bag_2) — is equivalent to creating a new bag_3 that is a copy of bag_1, then iterating through bag_2 and performing an insert into bag_3 for each occurance of each element of bag_2. In general, the update operators bundle together a sequence of inserts or removes, one for each occurrence of each element of one or more of the operands.

2.6.3.4 Type List<T>

Lists are ordered collections that allow duplicates. The elements of a list are ordered by the order of their insertion.

List<T> defines the property:

- current_position: Integer

List<T> refines the following operations inherited from type Collection:

- create () —> l: List<T>
- insert_element (o: T)
- select (predicate: String) —> l: List<T>

List<T> defines the following operations:

- insert_element_after (o: T, position: Integer)
- insert_element_before (o: T, position: Integer)
- insert_first_element (o: T)
- insert_last_element (o: T)
- remove_element_at (position: Integer)
- remove_first_element ()
- remove_last_element ()
- replace_element_at (o: T, position: Integer)
- retrieve_element_at (position: Integer) —> element: T
- retrieve_first_element () —> element: T
- retrieve_last_element () —> element: T

The current_position property of a list is set as a side effect of each insert, remove, replace, or retrieve operation executed on the list. Elements of a list are numbered 1 through o. An insert operation sets current_position to the number of the newly inserted element. A remove operation sets current_position to the number of the element preceding the element removed, unless the element removed was the first, in which case current_position is set to 1. Replace and retrieve operations both set current_position to the number of the element replaced or retrieved.

The insert_element operation inserts an element at the current position within the list. It is semantically an "insert_element_at" operation.

2.6.3.5 Type Array<T>

Arrays are one dimensional arrays of varying length. An initial size for the dimension is specified at array creation time. The length of the array can be either explicitly or implicitly changed after its creation. The array will be implicitly extended by assignments to array elements beyond the current end of the array.

Array<T> refines the following operations defined on Collection<T>.

- create (length:Integer) —> a: Array<T>
- insert_element_at (o: T, position: Integer)

Array<T> defines the following operations:

- insert_element_at (o: T, position: Integer)
- remove_element_at (position: Integer)
- replace_element_at (o: T, position: Integer)
- retrieve_element_at (position: Integer) —> element: T
- resize (new_size: Integer)

The remove_element_at operation replaces any current value contained in the cell of the array identified by position with nil. It does not remove the cell. This is in contrast to the remove_element_at operation defined on type List.

2.6.4 Built-in Type Structure

The model defines a built-in type generator Structure. A structure is an unnamed group of elements. Each element is a (name, value) pair, where the value may be any subtype of type Denotable_Object. Since structures and collections are subtypes of Denotable_Object, a structure may contain other structures or collections as the value of one or more of its elements.

Since structures are literals, they may occur as the value of attributes in an object interface declaration, e.g.,

```
interface Student {
...
    address: Structure<
        street_address: Structure<
            street_number: Integer
            street_name: String >
        city: String
        state: String
        zip: String>
    }
```

The operations defined by the type generator Structure<e1:T1, ... en:Tn) are the following:

- create([<initializer_list>]) —> s: Structure;
- delete()
- get_element_value (element) —> value: Denotable_Object
- set_element_value (element, value:Denotable_Object)
- clear_element_value (element)
- clear_all_values ()
- copy () —> s: Structure

The create operation returns a structure whose elements have optionally been initialized with values supplied in the <initializer_list>.

The copy operation returns a new structure with the same set of named elements as the initial structure, each of which has the same value as the initial structure. If the value of an element e1 in the initial structure was a literal, another copy of the literal is placed in the new structure. If the value of an element e2 in the initial structure was an object, then a reference to that object is placed in the corresponding element of the new structure. The corresponding elements of the two structures will now refer to a single instance of the referenced object. Copy semantics is "shallow copy".

2.7 Structured Literals

The model defines both atomic literals and structured literals. There are two subtypes of structured literal — Immutable_Collection and Immutable_Structure. The built-in subtypes of Immutable_Collection mirror the built-in subtypes of Collection:

- ❑ Immutable_Set
- ❑ Immutable_Bag
- ❑ Immutable_List
- ❑ Immutable_Array

There are no defined subtypes of Immutable_Structure.

Structured literals are created, but once they have been created, they cannot be modified. They do not have object identifiers that are visible at the level of the semantics of the model.

The assignment semantics for structured literals is copy on assignment. Assignment of an object of type Structured_Literal, or any of its subtypes, to another object will create a (logical) copy of the literal.

2.7.1 Immutable Collections

Immutable collections behave just like their mutable counterparts, except that they may not be modified. It is not possible to insert a member into an immutable collection or to remove a member from such a collection. Immutable sets are the basis for the extensional treatment of sets that is common in mathematical logic. We noted in Section 2.6 above that this is not consonant with the way most people think of sets in their everyday world, but it does have some use in limiting what are termed "view-update" problems in query languages. Consider the set s_1 defined as the union of sets s_2 and s_3. If s_1 is defined to be a mutable set then it is possible to insert a new member m into this set. But what does this mean? Since s_1 is the union of s_2 and s_3, m must presumably be a member of at least one of the sets s_2 and s_3. But which one? If s_2 and s_3 are insertion-defined sets, this may not be deducible from the properties of m.

The built-in types String and Bit_String are both subtypes of type List.

2.7.2 Immutable Structures

Immutable structures may be used to capture update constraints on the value of a property. They are also often returned as the result of queries — particularly interactive queries. The person (or program) that poses a query may not be interested in all of the properties of the objects that satisfy the query, but only in some of their properties. For efficiency reasons it may be preferable to have the query return newly created instances of an immutable structure type that has as its elements only the properties of interest, rather than collections of the objects as a whole. There is then no need for the requestor's program to walk through the objects, getting the values of the properties the requestor is interested in. Instead, tuples containing the values of those properties and no others may be returned directly.

The built-in types Date Time, and DateTime are subtypes of Immutable_Structure. These types carry the same semantics as the corresponding types in the SQL standard.

2.8 The Full Built-in Type Hierarchy

Figure 2-3 shows the full set of built-in types at the base of the type hierarchy.

The types shown in roman are directly instantiable. The types shown in italic are abstract types. They define characteristics that are inherited by their subtypes, but they cannot be instantiated in and of themselves. There can be nothing which is an instance of the parent type, but not an instance of one of these two subtypes.

We acknowledge the problem that types and type generators have been intermixed in the diagram. Formally a type generator such as Collection<T> cannot be a subtype of a type. Nor can a type be a subtype of a type generator, e.g., String shown as a subtype of List<T>. In the interests of simplicity, we have folded them into the same hierarchy in Figure 2-3.

- *Denotable_Object*
    - *Object*
        - Atomic_Object
            - Type
            - Exception
            - Iterator
        - *Structured_Object*
            - *Collection <T>*
                - Set <T>
                - Bag <T>
                - List <T>
                    - String
                    - Bit_String
                - Array<T>
            - Structure $<e_1:T_1 \ldots e_n:T_n>$
    - *Literal*
        - *Atomic_Literal*
            - Integer
            - Float
            - Character
            - Boolean
        - *Structured_Literal*
            - *Immutable_Collection <T>*
                - Immutable_Set <T>
                - Immutable_Bag <T>
                - Immutable_ List <T>
                    - Immutable_String
                    - Immutable_Bit_String
                - Immutable_Array<T>
                - Enumeration
            - Immutable_Structure $<e_1:T_1 \ldots e_n:T_n>$
                - Date
                - Time
                - DateTime
                - Interval
- *Characteristic*
    - *Property*
        - Attribute
        - Relationship
    - Operation

Figure 2-3. The Full Built-in Type Hierarchy

2.8.1 Access to the Metadata

All of the types shown in Figure 2-3 are instances of type Type. Type Type is itself both a subtype and an instance of type Atomic_Object. The *metadata* that defines the *schema* of a database is therefore accessible using the same operations that apply to user-defined types.

The metadata is exposed as a predefined subschema. The standard DML can be used to interrogate the metadata. This may occur at compile time, link time, load time, or execution time.

Type Type has the following instance properties:

- has_operations: Set<Operation>
- has_properties: Set<Property>
- has_subtypes: Set<Type>
- has_supertypes: Set<Type>
- name: String
- extent: Set<Atomic_Object>
- name_of_extent: String

Type Type defines the following operations:

- create_instance ([property=property_value{,property=property_value}]) —> o: Denotable_Object
- create_extent (name: String) —> c: Collection

Anything which is an instance of type Type will have particular operations and properties as the values of these type level properties. The type programmer can add additional operations and/or properties to subtypes of these built-in types.

2.8.2 Type Compatibility

The object model is strongly typed. Every denotable object has a type. Every operation requires typed operands. The rules for type identity and type compatibility are defined in the body of this subsection.

2.8.2.1 Type Compatibility among Objects

Two objects have the same type if and only if they have been declared to be instances of the same named type. Objects that have been declared to be instances of two different types are not of the same type, even if the types in question define the same set of properties and operations. Type compatibility for objects follows the subtyping relationships defined by the type hierarchy. If TS is a subtype of T, then an object of type TS can be assigned to an object of type T, but the reverse is not possible. No implicit conversions between objects are provided by the model.

2.8.2.2 Type Compatibility among Literals

Two atomic literals have the same type if they belong to the same set of literals, e.g., Integer, Float, ... Depending on programming language bindings, implicit conversions may be provided between the scalar literals, i.e., Integer, Float, Character, Boolean, Enum. Structured literals have the same type if at each level they have the same structure and each atomic part has the same type. A structured literal of type T can be assigned to a variable of type TS if and only if T and TS have the same structure at each level, and the type of each subobject of TS is the same as the corresponding type in T or else is a subtype of it. No implicit conversions are provided for structured literals.

2.9 Transactions

Programs that use persistent data are organized into *transactions*. Transactions are units of atomicity, consistency, and integrity. By *atomicity* we mean that the transaction either happens as a whole or not at all. If a transaction commits, then all of the changes made by that transaction are permanently installed in the database and made visible to other users of the database. If the transaction aborts, then none of the changes made by it are installed in the database, including those made prior to the time at which it aborted. By *consistency* we mean that a transaction is assumed to take the database from one internally consistent state to another internally consistent state. There may be points in time during the transaction when the database is internally inconsistent. However, no other user of the database sees changes made by a transaction until that transaction commits. This means that concurrent users of a shared database always see internally consistent versions of the database. By *integrity* we mean that once a transaction has committed, the DBMS guarantees that changes made by that transaction are never lost — this in spite of process abort, operating system failure, or hardware device failure.

The object model supports a nested transaction model, with dynamic scoping of transactions. Figure 2-4 illustrates a sequence of nested transactions:

```
Transaction::begin () —> t:Transaction
...
   Transaction::begin () —> x:Transaction
   ...
       Transaction::begin ()—>y:Transaction
           ...
           if minor_error y.abort ()
           if major_error y.abort_top_level ()
           ...
       y.commit ()
   ...
   x.commit()
...
t.commit ()
```

Figure 2-4. Nested Transactions

This figure shows a single outmost (or "top level") transaction t, that contains two nested transactions x and y. Changes made by t prior to beginning x are visible to x and

y. Changes made by x are visible to both its parent transaction t and its sibling transaction y once x commits. None of the changes made by x or y are visible outside of t, however, until t commits. Similiarly, if t aborts, then changes made by x and y will be aborted, whether or not they had already committed. The commit of a nested transaction is only relative to the commit of its containing parent transaction. If a nested transaction aborts, this does not cause abort of the containing transaction.

Nested transactions give the programmer a simple way of undoing changes made to shared persistent data. They also allow the DBMS to protect programs from network failures when operations are executed remotely. Each remote operation is implicitly executed within a nested transaction. If the operation cannot be completed, then it is only the nested transaction that is aborted, not the containing parent transaction.

The ODMG model uses a standard lock-based approach. Locks can be acquired on particular objects (although compliant implementations may actually either force or allow locks to be "escalated" to some higher level of physical granularity).

The ODMG model supports a traditional pessimistic concurrency control model as the default, though it does not preclude systems from supporting a wider range of concurrency control policies. This default model requires acquisition of a read lock on an object before it can be read and acquisition of a write lock on an object before that object can be modified. Readers of an object do not conflict with other readers, but writers conflict with both readers and writers. If there is a conflict, the holder of the lock proceeds, and the transaction that has requested the lock waits until the holder completes. The holder may complete either by committing or aborting, at which point locks are relinquished. Transactions subject to this protocol serialize in commit-order. All access, creation, modification, and deletion of persistent objects must be done within a transaction.

The operations defined on type Transaction are the following:

```
begin ([optimistic]) —> t: Transaction
commit ()
abort ()
checkpoint ()
abort_to_top_level ()
```

The begin operation creates and starts a transaction. Transactions must be explicitly created and started; they are not automatically started on database open or following a transaction commit or abort.

The commit operation causes all persistent objects created or modified during this transaction to become accessible to containing transactions, or if the transaction committing is a top-level transaction, to other transactions running against the database in other processes or threads. The transaction instance is deleted, and by default, all locks held by that transaction instance are released.

The abort operation causes the transaction instance to be deleted and the state of the database to be returned to the state it was in prior to the beginning of the transaction. All locks held by the transaction are released.

The checkpoint operation commits all modified objects to the database and retains all locks held by the transaction. It does not delete the transaction instance.

In the current standard, transient objects are not subject to transaction semantics. Aborting a transaction does not restore the state of modified transient objects.

As noted above, though, this model does include nested transactions; the operation abort_to_top_level causes nested transactions to be aborted to the topmost level.

The base model assumes a linear sequence of transactions within a single process running against a single logical database. It does not require (nor does it preclude) support for transactions that span multiple processes, or that span more than one logical database.

2.10 Operations on Type Database

A database provides storage for persistent objects of a given set of types. Each database has a *schema*. The schema consists of a set of type definitions. The database may contain instances of the types defined in its schema. A single (logical) database may be stored in one or more physical databases. This is an implementation issue that the model leaves open to implementors. Each database is an instance of the type Database. The type Database supports the following operations:

- open ()
- close ()
- contains_object? (oid:Object) —>b: Boolean
- lookup_object (oid: Object) —> b: Boolean

It may also support operations designed for database administration, e.g., move, copy, reorganize, verify, backup, restore, but these are also treated as implementation issues outside the realm of the object model.

The names of the types in the schema and their associated extents are global to the database, and become accessible to a program once it has opened the database. A database may also contain named objects, often called "root objects," that can be referenced by a program once it has opened the database. These three kinds of global names — type names, extent names, and root object names — provide entry points into the database, allowing the programmer to get an initial set of objects from which he can then navigate by following relationships or doing associative retrieval.

2.11 Subsequent Revisions of the ODMG Standard

The type hierarchy that serves as the structural skeleton for the ODMG-93 standard was designed to be strong enough to support increasing levels of functionality through a series of successive releases of the ODMG standard over the next ten years. In the interest of getting a standard that the major ODBMS vendors could support either at publication or soon thereafter, we have intentionally restricted the functionality supported by several of the types built into the ODMG-93 model. In many cases, however, we have a clear understanding of what additional functionality we want to support in a given area. We simply chose to defer that functionality to a later release of the standard. This section outlines the additional functionality that we expect to consider in the next release of the ODMG standard. It has been included for two reasons: first, to let reviewers of the base model know when functionality not present in the base model has been considered and simply deferred, and second, to allow implementors to begin developing pilot implementations in advance of the formal drafting process for ODMG-9X. This will hopefully give us a solid body of implementation experience on which to base our discussions about how much of the new functionality is ready for standardization, and what the detailed semantics of particular features should be.

The principal candidate functionality under consideration for the next release of the ODMG model is called out in the subsections that follow. The order of these subsections follows that of the base chapter. The presentation is intentionally brief.

2.11.1 Types/Instances/Extents

1. Multiple implementations are visible to the programmer. He may choose an implementation at object or characteristic creation time.
2. Indices may be dynamically created and destroyed at either the explicit request of the programmer or as the query processor decides they would be useful.
3. Multiple types may share one implementation.
4. The model allows declaration of instance properties that have type-defined values, e.g., the color attribute inherited from type Bird is defined to be 'red' for birds of subtype Cardinal.
5. It is possible to define named subextents of an object type. If a predicate determining the membership of an instance of this type in a particular subextent is specified in the type declaration, then the system will automatically maintain the subextent as well as or in lieu of the full extent.

2.11.2 Objects

1. An object may be an immediate instance of more than one type.
2. An object may dynamically acquire a type and dynamically lose a type. The simplest case of this is an object dynamically becoming an instance of a more immediate subtype of a type of which it is already an instance. The type programmer may override the system-supplied operations that implement this change, and/or may supply pre and post operations that the system will invoke. This can be used for complex integrity constraints.
3. An object may dynamically change representations. See item 1 under Section 2.11.2, above.
4. The lifetime of an object may be changed dynamically. Typical use is for a transient object to become persistent. Semantically this is straightforward, but it may be very difficult to achieve from an implementation point of view.
5. A fourth lifetime is introduced: coterminous_with_thread. This lifetime is longer than coterminus_with_procedure and shorter than coterminus_with_-process. It is designed to support operating systems that allow multiple threads of control within a single process.
6. Versions of objects are supported. Configurations containing specific versions of component objects are supported.
7. Versions of types are supported. Versions of the database schema are supported. Versions of subschemas may be supported.
8. Keys are supported. A key is a property or a set of properties that together uniquely identify the members of a collection. An object type may have more than one key.
9. The type programmer may extend or replace the set of built-in collection types. If a programmer-defined collection type supports the set of operations required by the query optimizer, then queries will work over these programmer-defined collections as well as over the built-in collection types.

2.11.3 Properties

2.11.3.1 Attributes

1. The type-definer may define properties of attributes.
2. Attribute types may participate in subtype/supertype relationships with other attribute types.
3. There is a richer set of declarative forms supporting common integrity constraints on values of attributes.

4. Attribute types may have attributes.
5. Attribute instances may have type-defined values.

2.11.3.2 Relationships

1. The type defined may define properties of relationships, e.g., transitive, reflexive, etc.
2. Relationship types may participate in subtype/supertype relationships with other relationship types.
3. There is built-in support for the consists_of relationship with predefined delete, move, copy, ... semantics.
4. The declaration of a one-to-many relationship, e.g., Professor.advisees: {Student}, implies the existence of a set of one-to-one relationships, e.g., Professor.{advisee:student}. Given an object p, the individual members of this set of relationships are distinguished not by unique names, but by the name or OID of the related object.
5. An object may acquire attributes by virtue of its participation in a relationship, e.g., Course.enrollment defines the number of students enrolled in a course. Student.course_load defines the number of courses the student is currently taking. Given the presence of one-to-many and sets of one-to-one relationships in the model (see item 4 above) model, this also introduces support for "indexed" attributes, e.g., Student.grade [in: Course].
6. The type definer may supply an implementation for a relationship type rather than using one of the built-in implementations. It is an open question at this point whether to allow overriding of a single operation or a subset of the operations predefined by the system as part of the built-in implementation of a relationship type. For complex constraint evaluation, the type-definer will be allowed to define pre and post operations.

2.11.4 Operations

1. Atomic operations are supported. These supercede separate Transaction::begin/commit/abort operations. Transaction::begin is an atomic operation call. Transaction::commit is the normal return of an atomic operation. Transaction::abort is treated as an exception return from the operation. Nested transaction semantics is achieved using nested operation calls.
2. Remote operations are supported. Execution of a remote operation automatically begins a nested transaction so that the calling operation is insulated from network failures.
3. Parallel operations may be supported.
4. Free-standing operations, not defined on a single type, are supported.

2.11.5 Transactions

1. A richer set of transaction protocols will be provided to support higher levels of concurrent access against a single shared database, to support long-lived transactions, and to support nomadic computing. These transaction protocols will build off of the the future model's support for versions of objects.

2. A single transaction may access objects in more than one database.

3. More than one process may participate in a single transaction.

4. A transaction may outlive the process that created it. This allows an engineer working on a complex design, for instance, to maintain a single unit of consistency over a period of days or weeks without having to have a process running continuously during that period to be the owner of a live transaction.

5. A process may also dynamically join and leave an existing transaction. This is useful in interactive design applications in which a designer has several processes active on his behalf at once.

6. Transaction consistency is made orthogonal to the question of the lifetime of an object. Transient objects may be transaction consistent as well as persistent objects. A transaction_consistent argument is added to the new operation. Abort of the transaction will delete transient as well as persistent objects created during the transaction. Transient objects modified during a transaction as well as persistent objects modified during the transaction will be returned to the state they were in prior to the beginning of the transaction.

2.11.6 Databases and Schema

1. The types Database, Schema, and Subschema will be introduced into the model. Each database has a single schema. However, several different databases may use the same schema. A schema is the set of all types whose instances may be stored in a single database. A subschema is a subset of the types in the schema. Access control and security will be defined on subschemas.

2. A subschema may include a subset of the types defined in the schema. Types and characteristics may be renamed in a subschema. Access control may be specified at the subschema level. The subschema may also leave out and therefore preclude use of some characteristics defined on the object types it includes. It is an open question whether new types unique to the subschema but not present in the schema may be included. If so, they will have to be types whose instances can be completely and unambiguously derived from instances of the types that are defined in the schema. These derived types will also have to be unambiguously updatable. Lock protocols have to be defined at the schema level so that applications using different subschemas interact consistently.

3. Type definitions are themselves treated as objects. The metadata is exposed as a predefined (sub)schema. The standard DML can be used to interrogate the metadata. This may occur at compile time, link time, load time, or execution time.

4. The types Interface and Implementation will be defined in the metadata.

Chapter 3

Object Definition Language

3.1 Introduction

The Object Definition Language (ODL) is a specification language used to define the interfaces to object types that conform to the ODMG Object Model. The primary objective of the ODL is to facilitate portability of database schemas across conforming ODBMSs. ODL also provides a step toward interoperability of ODBMSs from multiple vendors.

Several principles have guided the development of the ODL, including:

- ODL should support all semantic constructs of the ODMG Object Model
- ODL should not be a full programming language, but rather a specification language for interface signatures
- ODL should be programming-language independent
- ODL should be compatible with the OMG's Interface Definition Language (IDL)
- ODL should be extensible, not only for future functionality, but also for physical optimizations
- ODL should be practical, providing value to application developers, while being supportable by the ODBMS vendors within a relatively short time frame after publication of the specification.

ODL is not intended to be a full programming language. It is a specification language for interface signatures. Database management systems (DBMSs) have traditionally provided interfaces that support data definition (using a Data Definition Language — DDL) and data manipulation (using a Data Manipulation Language — DML). The DDL allows users to define their data types and interfaces. DML allows programs to create, delete, read, change, etc., instances of those data types. The ODL described in this chapter is a DDL for object types. It defines the characteristics of types, including their properties and operations. ODL defines only the signatures of operations and does not address definition of the methods that implement those operations. ODMG-93 does not provide a standard OML. Chapters 5 and 6 define standard APIs to bind conformant ODBMSs to C++ and to Smalltalk.

The ODL is intended to define object types that can be implemented in a variety of programming languages. Therefore ODL is not tied to the syntax of a particular programming language; users can use ODL to define schema semantics in a programming-language independent way. A schema specified in ODL can be supported by any ODMG-compliant ODBMS and by mixed-language implementations. This portability is necessary for an application to be able to run with minimal modification on a variety of ODBMSs. Some applications may in fact need simultaneous support from multiple ODBMSs. Others may need to access objects created and stored using different programming languages. ODL provides a degree of insulation for applications against the variations in both programming languages and underlying ODBMS products.

The C++ ODL and Smalltalk ODL bindings defined in Chapters 5 and 6 respectively are designed to fit smoothly into the declarative syntax of their host programming language. Due to the differences inherent in the object models native to these programming languages, it is not always possible to achieve consistent semantics across the programming-language specific versions of ODL. Our goal has been to minimize these inconsistencies, and we have noted in Chapters 5 and 6 the restrictions applicable to each particular language binding.

The syntax of ODL extends IDL —the Interface Definition Language developed by the OMG as part of the Common Object Request Broker Architecture (CORBA). IDL was itself influenced by C++, giving ODL a C++ flavor. Appendix B (ODBMS in the OMG ORB Environment) describes the relationship between ODL and IDL. ODL adds to IDL the constructs required to specify the complete semantics of the ODMG Object Model.

ODL also provides a context for integrating schemas from multiple sources and applications. These source schemas may have been defined with any number of object models and data definition languages; ODL is a sort of lingua franca for integration. For example, various standards organizations like STEP/PDES (EXPRESS), ANSI X3H2 (SQL), ANSI X3H7 (Object Information Management), CFI (CAD Framework Initiative), and others have developed a variety of object models and, in some cases, data definition languages. Any of these models can be translated to an ODL specification (Fig. 3-1). This common basis then allows the various models to be integrated with common semantics. An ODL specification can be realized concretely in an object programming language like C++ or Smalltalk.

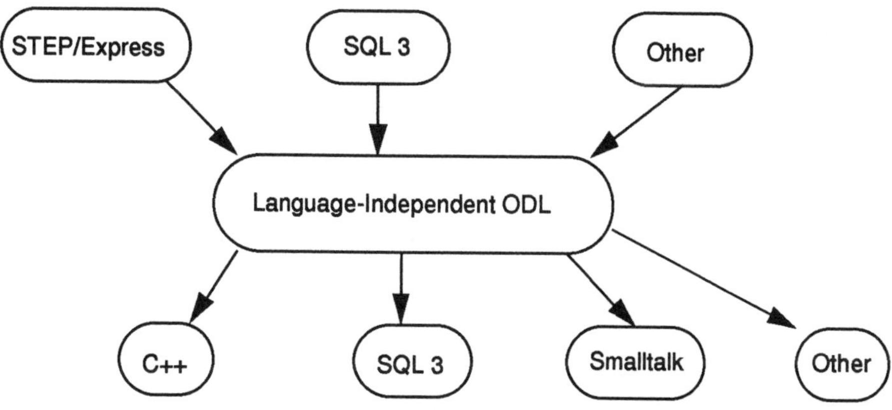

Figure 3-1: ODL Mapping to Other Languages

3.2 Specification

A type is defined by specifying its interface in ODL. The top-level BNF for ODL is as follows:

```
<type definition>    ::=  interface <type_name> [ : <supertype_list>]
                          {
                          [ <type_property_list> ]
                          [ <property_list> ]
                          [ <operation_list> ]
                          };
```

The characteristics of the type itself appear first, followed by lists that define the properties and operations of its interface. Any list may be omitted if it is not applicable in the interface.

3.2.1 Type Characteristics

Supertype information, extent naming, and specification of keys (i.e., uniqueness constraints) are all characteristics of types, but do not apply directly to the types' instances. The BNF for type characteristics follows.

```
<supertype_list>    ::=  <supertype> | <supertype>, <supertype_list>
<supertype>         ::=  <type_name>
<type_name>         ::=  <string>
<type_property_list>::=  <type_property>;
                          | <type_property> <type_property_list>
<type_property>     ::=  extent <extent_name>
                         | key[s] <key_list>
<extent_name>       ::=  <string>
<key_list>          ::=  <key_spec> | <key_spec> , <key_list>
<key_spec>          ::=  <property_name> | ( <property_list> )
<property_list>     ::=  <property_name>
                          | <property_name> , <property_list>
<property_name>     ::=  <attribute_name> | <traversal_path_name>
<attribute_name>    ::=  <string>
<traversal_path_name>
                    ::=  <string>
```

Each supertype must be specified in its own type definition. Each attribute or relationship traversal path named as (part of) a type's key must be specified in the property_list of the type definition. The supertype, extent, and key definitions may appear in any order in the type property list, and any may be omitted if inapplicable to the type being defined. A type definition should include no more than one extent or key definition.

A simple example for the interface definition of a Professor type is:

```
interface Professor:Person {
          extent professors;
          keys faculty_id, soc_sec_no;
      <property_list>
      <operation_list>
  };
```

3.2.2 Instance Properties

A type's instance properties are the attributes and relationships of its instances. These properties are specified in attribute and relationship specifications. The BNF follows.

```
<property_list>   ::=<property_spec>; | <property_spec> <property_list>
<property_spec>::=<attribute_spec> | <relationship_spec>
```

3.2.2.1 Attributes

The BNF for specifying an attribute follows.

```
<attribute_spec>     ::=  [ attribute ]
                          <domain_type> [ [<size> ] ] <attribute_name>
<domain_type>        ::=  <atomic_literal> | <structured_literal>
                          | <collection of objects or literals>
<size>               ::=  <integer>
```

For example, adding attribute definitions to the Professor type's ODL specification:

```
interface Professor:Person {
        extent professors;
            keys faculty_id, soc_sec_no;

        attribute string name;
        attribute Integer [6] faculty_id;
        Integer[10] soc_sec_no;
        Address address;
        attribute Set<struct<string degree_name,
                Year degree_year>> degrees;
        <operation_list>
};
```

The keyword **attribute** is optional. Entries in the attribute list have been shown in the example with and without the keyword. It is more likely that an ODL specifier would elect a convention and either always use the keyword **attribute** or never use it.

3.2.2.2 Relationships

A relationship specification names and defines a traversal path for a relationship. A traversal path definition includes designation of the target type, ordering information, and information about the inverse traversal path found in the target type. The BNF for relationship specification follows.

```
<relationship_spec> ::= [ relationship ]
                        <target_of_path> <traversal_path_name_1>
                        inverse <inverse_traversal_path>
                        [ { order_by <attribute_list> } ]
<traversal_path_name_1>
                    ::= <string>
```

```
<target_of_path>     ::=  <target_type>
                          | <collection_type> < <target_type> >
<target_type>        ::=  <type_name>
<inverse_traversal_path>::= <target_type> :: <traversal_path_name_2>
<traversal_path_name_2>
                     ::=  <string>
<attribute_list>     ::=  <attribute_name>
                          | <attribute_name>, <attribute_list>
```

Traversal path cardinality information is included in the specification of the target of a traversal path. The target type must be specified with its own type definition, unless the relationship is recursive. Use of the collection_type option of the BNF indicates cardinality greater than one on the target side. If this option is omitted, the cardinality on the target side is one. The most commonly used collection types are expected to be Set, for unordered members on the target side of a traversal path, and List, for ordered members on the target side. An ordering criterion is specified with the order_by clause. Each attribute used in an ordering criterion must be defined in the attribute list of the target type's definition. The inverse traversal path must be defined in the property list of the target type's definition.

For example, adding relationships to the Professor type's interface specification:

```
interface Professor: Person {
        extent professors;
        keys faculty_id, soc_sec_no;

        attribute string name;
        attribute Integer [6] faculty_id;
        Integer[10] soc_sec_no;
        Address address;
        attribute Set<struct<string degree_name,
                Year degree_year>> degrees;
        relationship Set<Student> advisees inverse Student::advisor;
         Set<TA> teaching_assistants inverse TA::works_for;
        relationship Department department
             inverse Department::faculty;
        <operation_list>
};
```

The keyword relationship is optional. Entries in the relationship list have been shown in the example with and without the keyword. It is more likely that someone using ODL would elect to either always use the keyword relationship or never use it.

Note that the attribute and relationship specifications can be mixed in the property list. It is not necessary to define all of one kind of property, then all of the other kind.

3.2.3 Operations

ODL is compatible with IDL for specification of operations. The high-level BNF for the <operation_list> follows.

```
<operation_list>      ::=  <operation_spec> ;
                           | <operation_spec>,<operation_list>
<operation_spec>      ::=  <return_type> <operation_name>
                           ( [<argument_list>] ) [<exceptions_raised>]
<return_type>         ::=  <type_name>
<operation_name>      ::=  <string>
<argument_list>       ::=  <argument>| <argument>, <argument_list>
<argument>            ::=  <role> [ < argument_name>: ] <argument_type>
<role>                ::=  in | out| inout
<exceptions_raised>::=     raises ( <exception_list>)
<exception_list>      ::=  <exception> | <exception>, <exception_list>
<exception>           ::=  [[ ... ]]
```

See Section 3.5 for the full BNF for operation specification.

3.3 An Example in ODL

This section illustrates the use of ODL to declare the schema for a sample application based on a university database. The object types in the sample application are shown as rectangles in Figure 3-2 below. Relationship types are shown as lines. The cardinality permitted by the relationship type is indicated by the arrows on the ends of the lines:

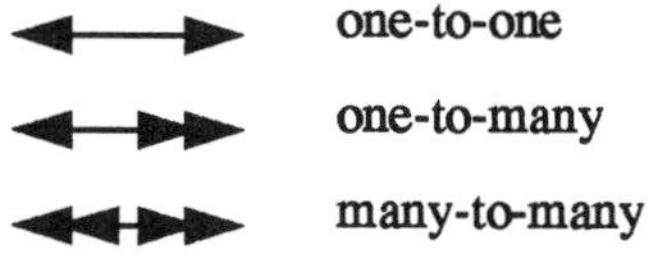

In the example, the type Professor is a subtype of the type Employee, and the type TA (for Teaching Assistant) is a subtype of both Employee and Student. Large gray arrows run from subtype to supertype in the figure.

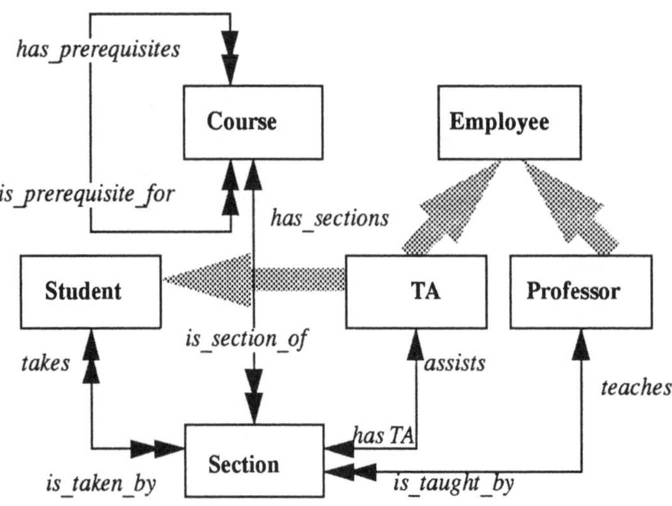

Figure 3-2 Graphical Representation of Schema

An ODL definition for the interfaces of the schema's types follows:

```
interface Course {
        extent courses;
        keys name, number;

        attribute string name;
        attribute string number;
        relationship List<Section> has_sections
            inverse Section::is_section_of
            {order_by Section::number};
        relationship Set<Course> has_prerequisites
            inverse Course::is_prerequisite_for;
        relationship Set<Course> is_prerequisite_for
            inverse Course::has_prerequisites;

        offer (in Semester) raises (already_offered);
        drop (in Semester) raises (not_offered);
}
```

```
interface Section {
        extent sections;
        key (is_section_of, number);

        attribute string number;
        relationship Professor is_taught_by inverse Professor::teaches;
        relationship TA has_TA inverse TA::assists;
        relationship Course is_section_of inverse Course::has_sections;
        relationship Set<Student> is_taken_by inverse Student::takes;
   ...
   }

interface Employee {
        extent employees;
        key (name, id);

        attribute string name;
        attribute Integer id;
          attribute annual_salary Integer;
          hire (in Person);
          fire (in Employee) raises (no_such_employee);
   }

interface Professor: Employee {
        extent professors;
           attribute enum rank {full, associate, assistant};
           relationship Set<Section> teaches inverse Section::is_taught_by;
           grant_tenure () raises (ineligible_for_tenure);
   }

interface TA:Employee, Student {
          relationship Section assists inverse Section::has_TA;

        ...
   }

interface Student {
        extent students;
        keys name, student_id;
```

```
        attribute string name;
        attribute string student_id;
        attribute struct<string college,string room_number> dorm_address;
        relationship Set<Section> takes inverse Section::is_taken_by;
        register_for_course (in Course, in Section)
            raises (unsatisfied_prerequisites, section_full, course_full);
        drop_course (in Course)
            raises (not_registered_for_that_course);
        assign_major (in Department);
        transfer (in from: Section, in to: Section)
            raises (section_full, not_registered_in_section);
    }
```

3.4 Another Example

Following is another example that will be used as an illustration of ODL. The same example will be used in Chapter 5 to illustrate the binding of ODL to C++. The application manages personnel records. The database manages information about people, their marriages, children, and history of residences. Person has an extent named people. A Person has name, address, spouse, children, and parents properties. The operations birth, marriage, ancestors, and move are also characteristics of Person: birth adds a new child to the children list of a Person instance, marriage defines a spouse for a Person instance, ancestors computes the set of Person instances who are the ancestors of a particular Person instance, and move changes a Person instance's address. An Address is a structure whose properties are number, street, and city: number is of type Integer, street is of type string, and city's value is a Ref to a City object. City has properties city_code, name, and population. City_code is of type Integer; name is of type string; population is a set of Refs to Person objects. Spouse is a traversal path to a spouse:spouse 1:1 recursive relationship; children is one of the traversal paths of a children:parents m:2 recursive relationship. The children of a given Person instance are ordered by birth_date. Parents is the other traversal path of the children:parents relationship.

The ODL specifying the interfaces for this schema follows.

```
    interface Person {
        extent people;

        attribute string name;
        attribute struct<Integer number, string street, Ref<City> city> address;
        relationship Person spouse inverse Person::spouse;
        relationship Set<Person> children inverse Person::parents
```

```
        {order_by birth_date} ;
    relationship Person[2] parents inverse Person::children;
    birth (in Person);
    marriage (in Person) raises (no_such_person);
    ancestors (out Set<Person>) raises (no_such_person);
    move (in Address);
    }
interface City {
    extent cities;
    key city_code;

    attribute Integer city_code;
    attribute string name;
    attribute Set<Ref<Person>> population;
 }
```

3.5 ODL Grammar

Following is the complete BNF for the ODL, which includes the IDL. The numbers on the production rules match their numbers in the OMG CORBA specification. Modified production rules have numbers suffixed by an asterisk, e.g., (5*). New production rules have alpha extensions, e.g., (5a).

```
(1)     <specification>::=<definition>
            | <definition> <specification>
(2)     <definition>::=<type_dcl>;
            |<const_dcl>;
            |<except_dcl>;
            |<interface>;
            |<module> ;
(3)     <module>::=module <identifier> {<specification>}
(4)     <interface>::=<interface_dcl>
            |<forward_dcl>
(5*)    <interface_dcl>::= <interface_header>
            [ : <persistence_dcl>] { [ <interface_body>] }
(5a)    <persistence_dcl>::= persistent | transient
(6)     <forward dcl>::=interface<identifier>
(7*)    <interface_header>::=
            interface<identifier> [<inheritance_spec>]
            [ <type_property_list> ]
(7a)    <type_property_list>
            ::=( [<extent_spec>] [<key_spec>] )
```

```
(7b)    <extent_spec>::= extent <string>
(7c)    <key_spec>::=key[s] <key_list>
(7d)    <key_list>::=<key> | <key> , <key_list>
(7e)    <key>::=<property_name> | ( <property_list> )
(7f)    <property_list>::=<property_name>
            | <property_name> , <property_list>
(7g)    <property_name>::=
            <attribute_name> | <traversal_path_name>
(7h)    <attribute_name>::= <string>
(7i)    <traversal_path_name>::=<string>
(8)     <interface_body>::=
            <export> | <export> <interface_body>
(9*)    <export>::=<type_dcl>;
            |<const_dcl>;
            |<except_dcl>;
            |<attr_dcl>;
            |<rel_dcl>;
            |<op_dcl>;
(10)    <inheritance_spec>::=
            :<scoped_name> [ , <inheritance_spec>]
(11)    <scoped_name>::=<identifier>
            |::<identifier>
            |<scoped_name>::<identifier>
(12)    <const_dcl>::=const <const_type> <identifier>=
            <const_exp>
(13)    <const_type>::=<integer_type>
            |<char_type>
            |<boolean_type>
            |<floating_pt_type>
            |<string_type>
            |<scoped_name>
(14)    <const_exp>::=<or_expr>
(15)    <or_expr>::=<xor_expr>
            |<or_expr>|<xor_expr>
(16)    <xor_expr>::=<and_expr>
            |<xor_expr>^<and_expr>
(17)    <and_expr>::=<shift_expr>
            |<and_expr>&<shift_expr>
(18)    <shift_expr>::=<add_expr>
            |<shift_expr>>><add_exp>
            |<shift_expr><<<add_expr>
(19)    <add_expr>::=<mult_expr>
            |<add_expr>+<mult_expr>
            |<add_expr>-<mult_expr>
```

```
(20)    <mult_expr>::=<unary_expr>
            |<mult_expr>*<unary_expr>
            |<mult-expr>/<unary_expr>
            |<mult_expr>%<unary_expr>
(21)    <unary_expr>::=<unary_operator><primary_expr>
            |<primary_expr>
(22)    <unary_operator>::=-
            |+
            |~
(23)    <primary_expr>::=<scoped_name>
            |<literal>
            |(<const_exp>)
(24)    <literal>::=<integer_literal>
            |<string_literal>
            |<character_literal>
            |<floating_pt_literal>
            |<boolean_literal>
(25)    <boolean_literal>::=TRUE
            |FALSE
(26)    <positive_int_const>::=<const_exp>
(27)    <type_dcl>::=typedef <type_declarator>
            |<struct_type>
            |<union_type>
            |<enum_type>
(28)    <type_declarator>::=<type_spec> <declarators>
(29)    <type_spec>::=<simple_type_spec>
            |<constr_type_spec>
(30)    <simple_type_spec>::=<base_type_spec>
            |<template_type_spec>
            |<scoped_name>
(31)    <base_type_spec>::=<floating_pt_type>
            |<integer_type>
            |<char_type>
            |<boolean_type>
            |<octet_type>
            |<any_type>
(32*)   <template_type_spec>::=<array_type>
            |<string_type>
(33)    <constr_type_spec>::=<struct_type>
            |<union_type>
            |<enum_type>
(34)    <declarators>::= <declarator>
            | <declarator> , <declarators>
(35)    <declarator>::=<simple_declarator>
```

|<complex_declarator>
(36) <simple_declarator>::=<identifier>
(37) <complex_declarator>::=<array_declarator>
(38) <floating_pt_type>::=**float**
|**double**
(39) <integer_type>::=<signed_int>
|<unsigned_int>
(40) <signed_int>::=<signed_long_int>
|<signed_short_int>
(41) <signed_long_int>::=**long**
(42) <signed_short_int>::=**short**
(43) <unsigned_int>::=<unsigned_long_int>
|<unsigned_short_int>
(44) <unsigned_long_int>::=**unsigned long**
(45) <unsigned_short_int>::=**unsigned short**
(46) <char_type>::=**char**
(47) <boolean_type>::=**boolean**
(48) <octet_type>::=**octet**
(49) <any_type>::=**any**
(50) <struct_type>::=**struct** <identifier> {<member_list>}
(51) <member_list>::=<member> | <member><member_list>
(52) <member>::=<type_spec><declarators>;
(53) <union_type>::=**union**<identifier>**switch**
(<switch_type_spec>) {<switch_body>}
(54) <switch_type_spec>::=<integer_type>
|<char_type>
|<boolean_type>
|<enum_type>
|<scoped_name>
(55) <switch_body>::=<case> | <case> <switch_body>
(56) <case>::=<case_label_list> <element_spec>;
(56a) <case_label_list>::=<case_label>
| <case_label> <case_label_list>
(57) <case_label>::=**case**<const_exp>:
|**default :**
(58) <element_spec>::=<type_spec><declarator>
(59) <enum_type>::=**enum**<identifier> { <enumerator_list>}
(59a) <enumerator_list>::=<enumerator>
| <enumerator> , <enumerator_list>
(60) <enumerator>::=<identifier>
(61*) <sequence_type>::=**Array** < <simple_type_spec>,
<positive_int_const>>
|**Array** <<simple_type_spec>>
(62) <string_type>::=**string** <<positive_int_const>>

```
                |string
(63)        <array_declarator>::=<identifier> <array_size_list>
(63a)       <array_size_list>::=<fixed_array_size>
                | <fixed_array_size> <array_size_list>
(64)        <fixed_array_size>::=[<postive_int_const>]
(65*)       <attr_dcl> ::= [readonly] [attribute]
                <domain_type> [<fixed_array_size> ]
                <attribute_name>
(65a)       <domain_type>::=<simple_type_spec>
                | <struct_type>
                | <enum_type>
                | <attr_collection_specifier> < literal>
                | <attr_collection_specifier> <identifier>
(65b)       <attr_collection_specifier>::= Set | List | Bag | Array
(65c)       <rel_dcl> ::= [relationship]
                <target_of_path>
                <traversal_path_name_1]
                inverse <inverse_traversal_path>
                [ { order_by <attribute_list> } ]
(65d)       <traversal_path_name_1>::= <string>
(65e)       <target_of_path>::=<identifier>
                | <rel_collection_type> <<identifer> >
(65f)       <inverse_traversal_path>::=
                <identifier> :: <traversal_path_name_2>
(65g)       <traversal_path_name_2>::=<string>
(65h)       <attribute_list>::=<attribute_name>
                | <attribute_name> , <attribute_list>
(65i)       <rel_collection_type::= Set | List
(66)        <except_dcl>::=exception <identifier>
                { [ <member_list>] }
(67)        op_dcl>::=[<op_attribute>]<op_type_spec>
                <identifier><parameter_dcls>
                [<raises_epr>][<context_expr>]
(68)        <op_attribute>::=oneway
(69)        <op_type_spec>::=<simple_type_spec>
                |void
(70)        <parameter_dcls>::=(<param_dcl> [<param_dcl_list>] )
                | ( )
(70a)       <param_dcl_list>::=<param_dcl>
                | <param_dcl> , <param_dcl_list>
(71)        <param_dcl>::=<param_attribute><simple_type_spec>
                <declarator>
(72)        <param_attribute>::=in
                |out
                |inout
```

(73) <raises_expr>::=**raises** (<scoped_name_list>)

(73a) <scoped_name_list>::=<scoped_name>
| <scoped_name> ,
<scoped_name_list>

(74) <context_expr>::=**context** (<string_literal_list>)

(74a) <string_literal_list>::=<string_literal>
| <string_literal> , <string_literal_list>

Chapter 4

Object Query Language

4.1 Introduction

In this chapter, we describe an object query language named OQL, which supports the ODMG data model. It is complete and simple. It deals with complex objects without privileging the set construct and the select-from-where clause.

We first describe the principles of the language in Section 4.2 followed by the input and result of a query in Section 4.3.

Section 4.4 deals with object identity and Section 4.5 gives a full description of the language: for each feature of the language, we give the syntax, an informal semantics, and an example.

The formal syntax is given in Section 4.6.

4.2 Principles

Our design is based on the following principles and assumptions:

- OQL is not computationally complete. It is a query language which provides easy access to an object database.
- OQL provides declarative access to objects.
- OQL relies on the ODMG object model.
- OQL has an abstract syntax.
- The formal semantics of OQL can easily be defined.
- OQL has one concrete syntax which is SQL-like, but it is easy to change the concrete syntax. Other concrete syntaxes are defined for merging the query language into programming languages (e.g., a syntax for preprocessed C++ and a syntax for Smalltalk).
- OQL provides high-level primitives to deal with sets of objects but does not restrict its attention to this collection construct. Thus, it also provides primitives to deal with structures and lists, and treats all such constructs with the same efficiency.
- OQL does not provide explicit update operators but relies on operations defined on objects for that purpose.
- OQL can be easily optimized by virtue of its declarative nature.

4.3 Query Input and Result

As a stand-alone language, OQL allows you to query denotable objects starting from their names, which act as entry points into a database. A name may denote any kind of object, i.e., atomic, structure, collection, or literal.

As an embedded language, OQL allows you to query denotable objects which are supported by the native language through expressions yielding atoms, structures, collections, and literals. An OQL query is a function which, when applied to this input, delivers an object whose type may be inferred from the operator contributing to the query expression. This point is illustrated with two short examples.

The schema defines the types Person and Employee. These types have the extents Persons and Employees respectively. One of these persons is the chairman (and there is an entry-point Chairman to that person). The type Person defines the name, birthdate, and salary as attributes and the operation age. The type Employee, a subtype of Person, defines the relationship subordinates and the operation seniority.

```
select distinct x.age
from x in Persons
where x.name = "Pat"
```

This selects the set of ages of all persons named Pat. Thus, this query returns a literal of type set<integer>.

```
select distinct struct(a: x.age, s: x.sex)
from x in Persons
where x.name = "Pat"
```

This does about the same, but for each person, it builds a structure containing age and sex. It returns a literal of type set<struct>.

```
select distinct struct(name: x.name, hps: (select y
                                           from y in x.subordinates
                                           where y.salary >100000))
from x in Employees
```

This is the same type of example, but now we use a more complex function. For each employee we build a structure with the name of the employee and the set of the employee's highly paid subordinates. Notice we have used a select-from-where clause in the select part. For each employee x, to compute hps, we traverse the relationship subordinates and select among this set the employees with a salary superior to $100,000. The result of this query is therefore a literal of the type set<struct>, namely:

```
set<struct (name: string, hps: bag<Employee>)>
```

We could also use a select operator in the from part:

```
select struct (a: x.age, s: x.sex)
from x in (select y from y in Employees where y.seniority ="10")
where x.name = "Pat"
```

Of course, you do not always have to use a select-from-where clause:

```
Chairman
```

Retrieves the Chairman object.

```
Chairman.subordinates
```

Retrieves the set of subordinates of the Chairman.

```
Persons
```

Gives the set of all persons.

4.4 Dealing with Object Identity

The query language supports both types of objects: mutable (i.e., having an OID) and literal (identity = their value), depending on the way these objects are constructed or selected.

4.4.1 Creating Objects

To create an object with identity a type name constructor is used. For instance, to create a Person defined in the previous example, simply write

```
Person(name: "Pat", birthdate: "3/28/56" , salary: 100,000)
```

The parameters in parenthesis allow you to initialize certain properties of the object. Those which are not explicitly initialized are given a default value.

You distinguish such a construction from the construction expressions that yield objects without identity. For instance,

```
struct (a: 10, b: "Pat")
```

creates a structure with two valued fields.

If you now return to the example in Section 4.3, instead of computing literals, you can build objects. For example, if you assume that the following mutable object types are defined:

```
type vectint: bag<integer>;
type stat
attributes
```

```
        a: integer
        s: char
    end_type;
    type stats: bag<stat>;
```

you can carry out the following queries:

```
vectint(select distinct x.age
        from x in Persons
        where x.name = "Pat")
```

which returns a mutable object of type vectint and

```
stats(select stat (a: x.age, s: x.sex)
      from x in Persons
      where x.name = "Pat")
```

which returns a mutable object of type stats.

4.4.2 Selecting Existing Objects

The extraction expressions may return

- A collection of objects with identity, e.g., select x from x in Persons where x.name ="Pat" returns a collection of persons whose name is Pat.
- An object with identity, e.g., element (select x from x in Persons where x.passport_number=1234567) returns the person whose passport number is 1234567.
- A collection of literals, e.g., select x.passport_number from x in Persons where x.name="Pat" returns a collection of integers giving the passport numbers of people named Pat.
- A literal, e.g., Chairman.salary.

Therefore the result of a query is an object with or without object identity: some objects are generated by the query language interpreter, and others produced from the current database.

4.5 Language Description

In this section, we use an example from the schema described in Chapter 3.

4.5.1 Queries

A query consists of a (possibly empty) set of query definition expressions followed by an expression. The set of query definition expressions is nonrecursive (although a query may call an operation which issues a query recursively).

Example:

```
define jones as select distinct x from x in Students where x.name = "Jones";
select distinct x.student_id from x in jones
```

This defines the set jones of students named Jones and gets the set of their student_ids.

4.5.2 Query Definition Expressions

If q is a query name and e is a query expression, then define q as e is a query definition expression which defines the query with name q.

Example:

```
define Does as select x from x in Student where x.name ="Doe"
```

This statement defines Does as a query returning a bag containing all the students whose name is Doe.

```
define Doe as element(select x from x in Student where x.name="Doe")
```

This statement defines Doe as a query which returns the student whose name is Doe (if there is only one, otherwise an exception is raised).

4.5.3 Elementary Expressions

- If x is a variable, then x is an expression.
- If a is an atom, then a is an expression. It defines the atom itself.

Example:

```
27
```

This query returns 27.

Example:

```
nil
```

This query returns the (non existing) object nil.

If e is a named object, then e is an expression. It defines the entity attached to the name.

Example:

```
Students
```

This query defines the set of students. We have assumed here that there exists a name Students corresponding to the extent of objects of the class Student.

If define q as e is a query definition expression, then q is an expression.

Example:

```
Doe
```

This query returns the student with name Doe. It refers to the query definition expression declared in Section 4.5.2.

4.5.4 Construction Expressions

4.5.4.1 Constructing Objects

If t is a type name, $p_1, p_2, ..., p_n$ are properties of t, and $e_1, e_2, ..., e_n$ are expressions, then t (p_1: e_1..., p_n: e_n) is an expression.

This defines a new object of type t whose properties $p_1, p_2, ..., p_n$ are initialized with the expression $e_1, e_2, ..., e_n$. The type of e_i must be compatible with the type of p_i.

If t is a type name of a collection and e is a collection literal, then t(e) is a collection object. The type of e must be compatible with t.

Examples:

```
Employee (name: "Peter", boss: Chairman)
```

Note that boss is a 1:N relationship. Therefore the creation of this new employee has a side effect on the object Chairman.

```
vectint (set(1,3,10))
```

This creates a mutable set object.

4.5.4.2 Constructing Structures

If $p_1, p_2, ..., p_n$ are property names, and $e_1, e_2, ..., e_n$ are expressions, then

struct (p_1: e_1, p_2: e_2, ..., p_n: e_n)

is an expression. It defines the structure taking values $e_1, e_2, ..., e_n$ on the properties $p_1, p_2, ..., p_n$.

Note that this dynamically creates an instance of the type struct(p_1: t_1, p_2: t_2, ..., p_n: t_n) if t_i is the type of e_i.

Example:

```
struct(name: "Peter", age: 25);
```

This returns a structure with two attributes name and age taking respective values Peter and 25.

4.5.4.3 Constructing Sets

If $e_1, e_2, ..., e_n$ are expressions, then set($e_1, e_2, ..., e_n$) is an expression. It defines the set containing the elements $e_1, e_2, ..., e_n$. It creates a set instance.

Example:

```
set(1,2,3)
```

This returns a set consisting of the three elements 1, 2, and 3.

4.5.4.4 Constructing Lists

If e_1, e_2, ..., e_n are expressions, then list(e1, e2, ..., en) is an expression. It defines the list having elements e_1, e_2, ..., e_n. It creates a list instance.

Example:

```
list(1,2,2,3)
```

This returns a list of four elements.

4.5.4.5 Constructing Bags

If e_1, e_2, ..., e_n are expressions, then bag(e_1, e_2, ..., e_n) is an expression. It defines the bag having elements e_1, e_2, ..., e_n. It creates a bag instance.

Example:

```
bag(1,1,2,3,3)
```

This returns a bag of five elements.

4.5.4.6 Constructing Arrays

If e_1, e_2, ..., e_n are expressions, then array(e_1, e_2, ..., e_n) is an expression. It defines an array having elements e_1, e_2, ..., e_n. It creates an array instance.

Example:

```
array(3,4,2,1,1)
```

This returns an array of five elements.

4.5.5 "Arithmetic" Expressions

4.5.5.1 Unary Expressions

If e is an expression and <op> is a unary operation valid for the type of e, then <op> e is an expression. It defines the result of applying <op> to e.

Example:

```
not(true)
```

This returns false.

4.5.5.2 Binary Expressions

If e_1 and e_2 are expressions and <op> is a binary operation, then e_1<op>e_2 is an expression. It defines the result of applying <op> to e_1 and e_2.

Example:

```
count(Students) - count(TA)
```

This returns the difference between the number of students and the number of TAs.

4.5.6 Collections Expressions

4.5.6.1 Universal Quantification

If x is a variable name, e_1 and e_2 are expressions, e_1 denotes a collection, and e_2 a predicate, then

for all x in e_1: e_2

is an expression. It returns true if all the elements of collection e_1 satisfy e_2 and false otherwise.

Example:

```
for all x in Students: x.student_id > 0
```

This returns true if all the objects in the Students set have a positive value for their student_id attribute. Otherwise it returns false.

4.5.6.2 Existential Quantification

If x is a variable name, if e_1 and e_2 are expressions, e_1 denotes a collection, and e_2 a predicate, then

exists x in e_1: e_2

is an expression. It returns true if there is at least one element of collection e_1 that satisfies e_2 and false otherwise.

Example:

```
exists x in Doe.takes: x.taught_by.name = "Turing"
```

This returns true if at least one course Doe takes is taught by someone named Turing.

4.5.6.3 Membership Testing

If e_1 and e_2 are expressions, e_2 is a collection, and e_1 has the type of its elements, then e_1 in e_2 is an expression. It returns true if element e_1 belongs to collection e_2.

Example:

```
Doe in Does
```

This returns true.

```
Doe in TA
```

This returns true if Doe is a Teaching Assistant.

4.5.6.4 Select From Where

If e, e', e_1, e_2, ..., e_n are expressions, and x_1, x_2, ..., x_n are variable names, then

select e from x_1 in e_1, x_2 in e_2 ..., x_n in e_n where e' and

select distinct e from x_1 in e_1, x_2 in e_2 ..., x_n in e_n where e'

are expressions.

The result of the query is a set for a select distinct or a bag for a select.

If you assume e_1, e_2, ..., e_n are all set and bag expressions, then the result is obtained as follows: take the cartesian product[1] of the sets e_1, e_2, ..., e_n; filter that product by expression e' (i.e., eliminate from the result all objects that do not satisfy boolean expression e'); apply the expression e to each one of the elements of this filtered set and get the result. When the result is a set (distinct case) duplicates are automatically eliminated.

The situation where one or more of the collections e_1, e_2, ..., e_n is an indexed collection is a little more complex. The select operator first converts all these collections into sets and applies the previous operation. The result is a set (distinct case) or else a bag. So, in this case, we simply transform each of the e_i's into a set and apply the previous definition.

Example:

```
select couple(student: x.name, professor: z.name)
    from x in Students,
        y in x.takes,
        z in y.taught_by
where z.rank = "full professor"
```

This returns a bag of objects of type couple giving student names and the names of the full professors from which they take classes.

4.5.6.5 Sort-by Operator

If e is an expression and e_1, e_2, ..., e_n are expressions with x a free variable then sort x in e by e_1, e_2, ..., e_n is an expression. It returns a list of elements of e sorted lexicographically by the functions e_1, e_2, ..., e_n.

Example:

```
sort x in Persons by x.age, x.name
```

---

1. The Cartesian product between a set and a bag is defined by first converting the set into a bag, and then get the resulting bag, which is the Cartesian product of the two bags.

This sorts the set of persons on their age, then on their name and puts the sorted objects into the result as a list.

4.5.6.6 Unary Set Operators

If e is an expression which denotes a collection, if <op> is an operator from {min, max, count, sum, avg}, then <op>(e) is an expression.

Example:

```
max (select x.salary from x in Professors)
```

This returns the maximum salary of the Professors.

4.5.6.7 Group-by Operator

If e is an expression which denotes a collection, $p_1, p_2, ..., p_n$ are property names, $e_1, e_2, ..., e_n$ are expressions with x a free variable, $p'_1, p'_2, ..., p'_m$ are property names, and $e'_1, e'_2, ..., e'_m$ are expressions with *partition* a free variable, then

$$\text{group } x \text{ in } e \text{ by } (p_1: e_1, p_2: e_2, ..., p_n: e_n)$$

is an expression and

$$\text{group } x \text{ in } e \text{ by } (p_1: e_1, p_2: e_2, ..., p_n: e_n) \text{ with } (p'_1: e'_1, a'_2: e'_2, ..., p'_m: e'_m)$$

is an expression.

The first form yields a set of structures. Each structure stands for a particular partition of e according to the partition criteria given by the by clause. Therefore, each structure has the valued properties for this partition, completed by a property which is conventionally called *partition* and which is the set of all objects matching this particular valued partition.

Example:

```
group x in Employees
by ( low: x.salary < 1000,
   medium:x.salary >= 1000 and x.salary < 10000,
  high:   x.salary >= 10000)
```

This gives a set of three elements, each of which has a property called partition which contains the set of employees that enter in this category. So the type of the result is:

```
set<struct(low: boolean, medium: boolean, high: boolean,
           partition: set<Employee>)>
```

The second form enhanced the first one by the with clause which enables one to compute the result using aggregate functions which operate on each partition. The result is a set of structures creating a partition of e, according to the partition criteria.

Each structure comes with the properties of the by clause plus the properties of the with clause.

Example:

```
group e in Employees
by (department: e.deptno)
with (avg_salary: avg(select x.salary from x in partition))
```

This gives a set of couples: department and average of the salaries of the employees working in this department. So the type of the result is:

```
set<struct(department: integer, avg_salary: float)>
```

4.5.7 Indexed Collection Expressions

4.5.7.1 Getting the i-th Element of an Indexed Collection

If e_1 and e_2 are expressions, e_1 is a list or an array, e_2 is an integer, then $e_1[e_2]$ is an expression. This extracts the e_2-th element of the indexed collection e_1. Notice that the first element has the rank 0.

Example:

```
list (a,b,c,d) [1]
```

This returns b.

Example:

```
element (select x
            from x in course
            where x.name = "math" and x.number ="101").requires[2]
```

This returns the third prerequisite of Math 101.

4.5.7.2 Extracting a Subcollection of an Indexed Collection.

If e_1, e_2, and e_3 are expressions, e_1 is a list or an array, and e_2 and e_3 are integers, then $e_1[e_2:e_3]$ is an expression. This extracts the subcollection of e_1 starting at position e_2 and ending at position e_3.

Example:

```
list (a,b,c,d) [1:3]
```

This returns list (b,c,d).

Example:

```
element (select x
            from x in course
```

```
where x.name="math" and x.number="101").requires[0:2]
```

This returns the list consisting of the first three prerequisites of Math 101.

4.5.7.3 Getting the First and Last Elements of a Collection

If e is an expression, <op> is an operator from {first, last}, and e is a list or an array, then <op>(e) is an expression. This extracts the first and last element of a collection.

Example:

```
first(element(select x
              from x in course
              where x.name="math" and x.number="101").requires)
```

This returns the first prerequisite of Math 101.

4.5.7.4 Concatenating Two Indexed Collections

If e_1 and e_2 are expressions and e_1 and e_2 are both lists or both arrays, then e_1+e_2 is an expression. This computes the concatenation of e_1 and e_2.

```
list (1,2) + list( 2,3)
```

This query generates list (1,2,2,3).

4.5.8 Binary Set Expressions

If e_1 and e_2 are expressions, if <op> is an operator from {union, except, intersect}, if e_1 and e_2 are sets or bags, then e_1 <op> e_2 is an expression. This computes set theoretic operations, union, difference, and intersection on e_1 and e_2, as defined in Chapter 2.

When the operand's collection types are different (bag and set), the set is first converted into a bag and the result is a bag.

Examples:

```
Student except Ta
```

This returns the set of students who are not Teaching Assistants.

```
bag(2,2,3,3,3) union bag(2,3,3,3)
```

This bag expression returns bag(2,2,3,3,3,2,3,3,3)

```
bag(2,2,3,3,3) intersect bag(2,3,3,3)
```

The intersection of 2 bags yields a bag that contains the maximum for each of the duplicate values. So the result is: bag(2,2,3,3,3)

```
bag(2,2,3,3,3) except bag(2,3,3,3)
```

This bag expression returns bag(2).

4.5.9 Structure Expressions

4.5.9.1 Extracting an Attribute or Traversing a Relationship from an Object

If e is an expression, if p is a property name, then e->p and e.p are expressions. These are alternate syntax to extract property p of an object e.

If e happens to designate a deleted or a non existing object, i.e. nil, an attempt to access the attribute or to traverse the relationship raises an exception. However, a query may test explicitly if an object is different from nil before accessing a property.

Example:

```
Doe.name
```

This returns Doe.

Example:

```
Doe->spouse != nil and Doe->spouse->name = "Carol"
```

This returns true, if Doe has a spouse whose name is Carol, or else false.

4.5.10 Conversion Expressions

4.5.10.1 Extracting the Element of a Singleton

If e is a collection-valued expression, element(e) is an expression. This takes the singleton e and returns its element. If e is not a singleton this raises an exception.

Example:

```
element(select x from x in Professors where x.name ="Turing")
```

This returns the professor whose name is Turing (if there is only one).

4.5.10.2 Turning a List into a Set

If e is a list expression, listtoset(e) is an expression. This converts the list into a set, by forming the set containing all the elements of the list.

Example:

```
listtoset (list(1,2,3,2))
```

This returns the set containing 1, 2, and 3.

4.5.10.3 Flattening Collection of Collections

If e is a collection-valued expression, flatten(e) is an expression. This converts a collection of collections of t into a collection of t. So this flattening operates at the first level only.

Assuming the type of e to be col1<col2<t>>, the result of flatten(e) is:

- If col2 is a set (resp. a bag), the union of all col2<t> is done and the result is a set<t> (resp. bag<t>).
- If col2 is a list (resp. an array) and col1 is a list (resp. an array) as well, the concatenation of all col2<t> is done following the order in col1 and the result is col2<t>, which is thus a list (resp. an array). Of course duplicates, if any, are maintained by this operation.
- If col2 is a list or an array and col1 is a set or a bag, the lists or arrays are converted into sets, the union of all these sets is computed, and the result is a set<t>, therefore without duplicates.

Examples:

```
flatten(list(set(1,2,3), set(3,4,5,6), set(7)))
```

This returns the set containing 1,2,3,4,5,6,7.

```
flatten(list(list(1,2), list(1,2,3)))
```

This returns list(1,2,1,2,3).

```
flatten(set(list(1,2), list(1,2,3)))
```

This returns the set containing 1,2,3.

4.5.10.4 Typing an Expression

If e is an expression and c is a type name, then (c)e is an expression. This asserts that e is an object of class type c.

If it turns out that it is not true, an exception is raised at runtime. This is useful to access a property of an object which is statically known to be of a superclass of the specified class.

Example:

```
select ((Employee) s).salary
from s in Students
where s in (select sec.assistant from sec in Sections)
```

This returns the set of salaries of all students who are teaching assistants, assuming that Students and Sections are the extents of the classes Student and Section.

4.5.11 Object Expressions

4.5.11.1 Applying an Operation to an Object

If e is an expression and f is an operation name, then e->f and e.f are expressions. These are alternate syntax to apply on operation on an object.

Example:

jones->number_of_students

This applies the operation number_of_students to jones.

4.5.11.2 Applying an Operation with Parameters to an Object

If e is an expression, if e_1 , e_2 , ..., e_n are expressions and f is an operation name, then e->f(e_1, e_2, ..., e_n) and e.f(e_1, e_2, ..., e_n) are expressions that apply operation f with parameters e_1, e_2, ..., e_n to object e.

In both cases, if e happens to designate a deleted or a nonexisting object, i.e. nil, an attempt to apply an operation to it raises an exception. However, a query may test explicitly if an object is different from nil before applying an operation.

4.6 OQL BNF

The OQL grammar is given using a rather informal BNF notation.

- { symbol } means a sequence of 0 or n symbol(s).
- [symbol] means an optional symbol.
- **keyword** is a terminal of the grammar.
- xxx_name has the syntax of an identifier.
- xxx_literal is self-explanatory, e.g., "a string" is a string_literal.
- bind_argument stands for a parameter when embedded in a programming language, e.g., $3i.

4.6.1 Axiom

query_program ::= {define_query;} query
define_query ::= **define** identifier **as** query

4.6.1.1 Basic

query ::= **nil**
query ::= **true**
query ::= **false**
query ::= integer_literal
query ::= float_literal
query ::= character_literal
query ::= string_literal
query ::= entry_name
query ::= query_name
query ::= bind_argument[2]
query ::= (query)

4.6.1.2 Arithmetic

query ::= query + query[3]

query ::= query - query
query ::= query * query
query ::= query / query
query ::= - query
query ::= query **mod** query
query ::= **abs** (query)

4.6.1.3 Comparison

query ::= query = query
query ::= query != query
query ::= query < query
query ::= query <= query
query ::= query > query
query ::= query >= query

4.6.1.4 Boolean Expression

query ::= **not** query
query ::= query **and** query
query ::= query **or** query

4.6.1.5 Constructor

query ::= **type_name** (*[*query*]*)
query ::= **type_name** (identifier:query {,ident:query})
query ::= **struct** (identifier: query {, identifier: query})
query ::= **set** (*[*query {, query}*]*)
query ::= **bag** (*[*query {,query}*]*)
query ::= **list** (*[*query {,query}*]*)
query ::= **array** (*[*query {,query}*]*)

4.6.1.6 Accessor

query ::= query dot attribute_name
query ::= query dot relationship_name
query ::= query dot operation_name([query {,query}])
dot ::= **.** | **->**

query ::= query [query]
query ::= query [query:query]
query ::= **first** (query)
query ::= **last** (query)

---

[2] A bind argument allows one to bind expressions from a programming language to a query when embedded into this language (see chapters on language bindings).

[3] The operator + is also used for list and array concatenation.

4.6.1.7 Conversion

query ::= **listtoset** (query)
query ::= **element** (query)
query ::= **flatten** (query)
query ::= (class_name) query

4.6.1.8 Set Expression

query ::= query **intersect** query
query ::= query **union** query
query ::= query **except** query

4.6.1.9 Collection Expression

query ::= **for all** identifier **in** query: query
query ::= **exists** identifier **in** query: query
query ::= query **in** query
query ::= **select** [**distinct**] query
from identifier **in** query
{, identifier **in** query}
[**where** query]
query ::= **sort** identifer **in** query
by query {, query}
query ::= **count** (query)
query ::= **sum** (query)
query ::= **min** (query)
query ::= **max** (query)
query ::= **avg** (query)
query ::= **group** identifier **in** query
by (identifier: query {,identifier: query})
[**with** (identifier: query {,identifier: query})]

Chapter 5

C++ Binding

5.1 Introduction

This chapter defines the C++ binding for ODL/OML.

ODL stands for Object Definition Language. It is the declarative portion of C++ ODL/OML. The C++ binding of ODL is expressed as a class library and an extension to the standard C++ class definition grammar. The class library provides classes and functions to implement the concepts defined in the ODMG object model. The extension consists of a single additional keyword and associated syntax that add declarative support for relationships to the C++ class declaration. OML stands for Object Manipulation Language. It is the language used for retrieving objects from the database and modifying them. The C++ OML syntax and semantics are those of standard C++ in the context of the standard class library.

ODL/OML specifies only the logical characteristics of objects and the operations used to manipulate them. It does not discuss the physical storage of objects. It does not address the clustering or memory management issues associated with the stored physical representation of objects or access structures like indices used to accelerate object retrieval. In an ideal world these would be transparent to the programmer. In the real world they are not. An additional set of constructs called *physical pragmas* is defined to give the programmer some direct control over these issues, or at least to enable a programmer to provide "hints" to the storage management subsystem provided as part of the ODBMS runtime. Physical pragmas exist within the ODL and OML. They are added to object type definitions specified in ODL, expressed as OML operations, or shown as optional arguments to operations defined within OML. Because these pragmas are not in any sense a stand-alone language, but rather a set of constructs added to ODL/OML to address implementation issues, they are included within the relevant subsections of this chapter.

The chapter is organized as follows. Section 5.2 discusses the ODL. Section 5.3 discusses the OML. Section 5.4 discusses OQL — the distinguished subset of OML that supports associative retrieval. Associative retrieval is retrieval based on the values of the properties of objects rather than on their IDs or names. Section 5.5 provides an example program. Section 5.6 defines a C++ ODL/OML binding we plan to offer in the future when it is practical to do so.

5.1.1 Language Design Principles

The programming language-specific bindings for ODL/OML defined in Chapters 5 and 6 of this document, for C++ and Smalltalk respectively, are based on one basic principle: The programmer feels that there is one language, not two separate languages with arbitrary boundaries between them. This principle has four corollaries that are evident in the design of the C++ binding defined in the body of this chapter:

1. There is a single unified type system across the programming language and the database; individual instances of these common types can be persistent or transient.
2. The programming language-specific binding for ODL/OML respects the syntax and semantics of the base programming language into which it is being inserted.
3. The binding is structured as a small set of additions to the base programming language; it does not introduce sublanguage-specific constructions that duplicate functionality already present within the base language.
4. Expressions in the OML compose freely with expressions from the base programming language and vice versa.

5.1.2 Language Binding

The C++ to ODBMS language binding approach described by this standard is based on the smart pointer or "Ref-based" approach.

In a Ref-based approach, the C++ binding maps the Object Model into C++ by introducing a set of classes that can have both persistent and transient instances. These classes are informally referred to as "persistence-capable classes" or "database classes" in the body of this chapter. These classes are distinct from the normal classes defined by the C++ language, all of whose instances are transient; that is, they don't outlive the execution of the process in which they were created. Where it is necessary to distinguish between these two categories of classes, the former are called "database-capable classes"; the latter are referred to as "C++ classes." For each database class X, an ancillary class Ref<X> is automatically defined by the ODL preprocessor. Instances of database classes are then referenced using parameterized references, e.g.,

```
(1) Ref<Professor> profP;
(2) Ref<Department> deptRef;
(3) profP—>grant_tenure();
(4) deptRef = profP—>dept;
```

Statement (1) declares the object profP as an instance of the automatically defined type Ref<Professor>. Statement (2) declares deptRef as an instance of the automatically defined type Ref<Department>. Statement (3) invokes the grant_tenure() operation defined on class Professor, on the instance of that class referred to by profP. Statement (4) assigns the value of the dept attribute of the professor referenced by profP to the variable deptRef.

Instances of database classes may contain occurrences of C++ built-in types or user--defined classes. However, they may refer to such classes (using C++ pointers (*) or C++ references (&)) only during execution of a transaction. At the time a transaction is committed, there must either be no such references within objects committed to persistent storage, or such references must be set to NULL by the Transaction::commit() operation.

In this chapter we use the following terms to describe the places where the standard is formally considered undefined or allows for an implementor of one of the bindings to make implementation-specific decisions with respect to implementing the standard. The terms are:

> *Undefined:* The behavior is unspecified by the standard. Implementations have complete freedom (can do anything or nothing), and the behavior need not be documented by the implementor or vendor.
>
> *Implementation-defined:* The behavior is specified by each implementor/vendor. The implementor/vendor is allowed to make implementation-specific decisions about the behavior. However, the behavior must be well defined and fully documented and published as part of the vendor's implementation of the standard.

Figure 5-1 shows the hierarchy of languages involved, as well as the preprocess, compile, and link steps that generate an executable application.

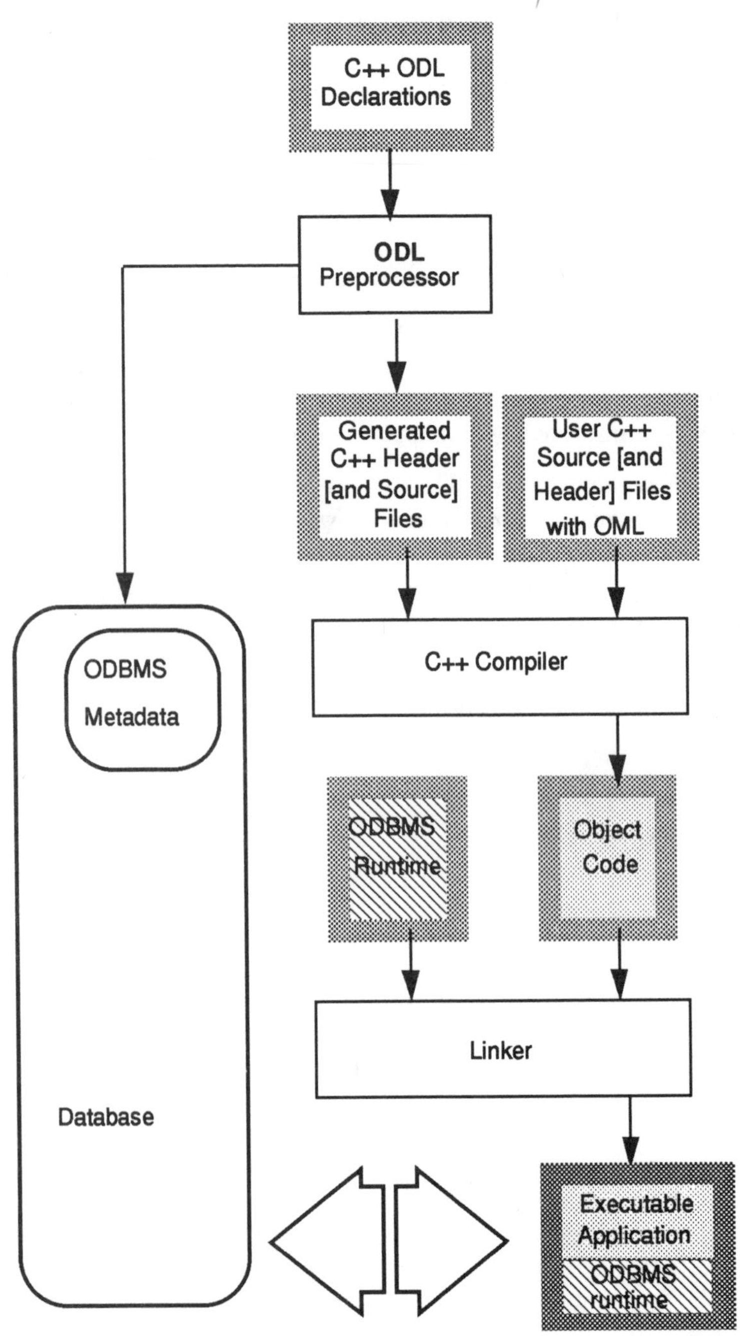

Figure 5-1 Language Hierarchy

5.1.3 Mapping the ODMG Object Model into C++

Although C++ provides a powerful data model that is close to the one presented in Chapter 2, it is worth trying to explain more precisely how concepts introduced in Chapter 2 map into concrete C++ constructions.

5.1.3.1 Object and Literal

An ODMG object type maps into a C++ class. Depending on how a C++ class is instantiated, the result can be an ODMG object or an ODMG literal. A C++ object embedded into a top-level class acts as an ODMG literal. This is explained by the fact that a block of memory is inserted into the top-level object and belongs entirely to it. For instance, one cannot copy the top-level object without getting a copy of the embedded one at the same time. In this sense the embedded object cannot be considered as having an identity, since it acts as an immutable literal.

As a general rule one can implement an ODMG object by a reference to a C++ object.

5.1.3.2 Relationship

This concept is not supported as such by C++ and must be simulated by the support of automatically generated C++ methods that implement it.

The relation itself is implemented as a reference (one-to-one relation) or as a collection (one-to-many relation) embedded in the object.

5.1.3.3 Extents

This is not directly supported by C++. The programmer is responsible for defining a collection and writing methods that maintain it.

5.1.3.4 Keys

Key declarations are not supported by C++. Here again these can be simulated by standard C++ data members with associated code and index data structure to manage them.

5.1.3.5 Names

In the C++ binding an object can acquire only one name, while in the ODMG model more than one name may refer to the same object.

5.1.3.6 Implementation

C++ has implicitly this notion of dividing an object into two parts: its definition (public part) and its implementation (private part and method bodies). However, only one implementation is possible in C++ for a definition.

5.1.3.7 Array

C++ provides a syntax for creating and accessing a contiguous and indexable sequence of objects. This has been chosen to map partially to the ODMG Array collection. To complement it, a Varray C++ class is also provided, which implements an array whose bounds may vary with time.

5.1.3.8 Database Administration

Some operations regarding database administration are intentionally omitted from the C++ binding. For instance the C++ binding does not provide a means to create a database nor to define an index on a collection.

5.2 C++ ODL

This section defines the C++ Object Definition Language. C++ ODL provides a description of the database schema as a set of object classes — including their attributes, relationships, and operations — in a syntactic style that is consistent with that of the declarative portion of a C++ program. Instances of these classes can be manipulated through the C++ OML.

Following is an example declaring type Professor. New keywords (not defined by C++) are shown in bold.

```
class Professor : public  Pobject
{
    public:
        // properties:
            int age;
            int id_number;
            char* office_number;
            char* name;
            Ref<Department>  dept  inverse professors;
            Set<Student> advisees  inverse Student::advisor;
        // operations:
            void grant_tenure ();
            void assign_course (course);

    private:
        ...
}
```

Operation declarations are identical to C++ *member function* declarations. Property declarations are similar to C++ *data member* declarations. The Object Model defines two subtypes of property — attribute and relationship. Relationship declarations are syntactically distinguished from C++ data member declarations by the presence of the inverse clause. Attribute declarations are syntactically distinguished from C++ data member declarations only in the event that they have a computed value rather than a stored value.

The syntax used in defining the BNF in the following sections is:

plain font	nonterminal
bold font	terminal
[symbol]	optional
{symbol}	zero or more
a | b	a or b
<<C++>>	nonterminal, standard C++

Nonterminals that are not defined but which have an obvious usage, e.g., class_name, are not defined here. Their syntax can be inferred from their names or from standard C++ usage.The syntax and semantics of C++ are adopted in their entirety, with the addition of a few keywords, which are explained in the following sections.

The BNF of basic class declarations then is:

```
class_declaration ::=class class_name [:supertype_list]
            {
            instance_characteristics_block
            };
supertype_list::= <<C++>>
instance_characteristics_block ::= public: characteristic;{characteristic;}
characteristic ::= property | operation
property       ::= attribute | relationship_traversal_path
operation      ::= <<C++>>
```

Supertypes are specified using the standard C++ syntax within the class header, e.g., class Professor : public Person.

5.2.1 Attribute Declarations

Attribute declarations are syntactically identical to data member declarations within C++. Because notions of attributes as objects are not yet defined and included in this standard, attributes and data members are not and cannot be syntactically distinguished. In this standard, an attribute cannot have properties (e.g., unit of measure) and there is no way to specialize the get_value and set_value operations defined on the built-in type attribute (e.g., to raise an event when a value is changed).

The BNF for an attribute declaration is:

```
attribute           ::=  literal_type_name attribute_name;
literal_type_name   ::=  atomic_literal_type_name
                         | structured_literal_type_name
boolean             ::=  char;
date                ::=  ; // not defined yet
time                ::=  ; // not defined yet
```

```
date_time              ::=  ; // not defined yet
interval               ::=  ; // not defined yet
string                 ::=  ; // not defined yet
binary                 ::=  ; // not defined yet
atomic_literal_type_name
                       ::=  int | long | short | float | double | boolean
structured_literal_type
                       ::=  char* | date | time | date_time | interval
                            | string | binary | struct_definition
                            | Collection<literal_type_name>
struct_definition      ::=  <<C++>>
```

Examples:

```
class Student: public Pobject {
   public:
      char * name;
      Telephone_number dorm_phone;
      struct {int PO_box,
          char * university,
          char * city
          char * state
          char * zip_code} university_address;
      List<char*> favorite_friends;
   }
```

The attribute name takes a pointer to a character string as its value. The attribute dorm_phone takes a user-defined literal type Telephone_number as its value. The attribute university_address takes a structure. The Object Model notion of a *structure* maps into the C++ construct *struct* or *class* embedded in a class. The attribute favorite_friends takes a list of character strings as its value.

5.2.2 Relationship Declarations

Relationship types do not have syntactically separate type definitions. Instead, the *traversal paths* used to cross relationships are defined within the bodies of the definitions of each of the two object types that fill a role in the relationship type. For example, if there is a one-to-many relationship between professors and the students they have as advisees, then the traversal path advisees is defined within the type definition of the object type Professor, and the traversal path advisor is defined within the type definition of the object type Student. The relationship itself does not have a separate type declaration.

A traversal path declaration is distinguished from an attribute declaration by the required presence of the inverse keyword. The BNF for relationship traversal path declaration is:

```
relationship_traversal_path ::= to1_traversal_path | toN_traversal_path
to1_traversal_path  ::=  object_type_name traversal_path_name
                         inverse [object_type_name::]
                         inverse_traversal_path_name;
toN_traversal_path  ::=  path_type traversal_path_name
                         inverse [object_type_name::]
                         inverse_traversal_path_name;
path_type           ::=  collection_type <Ref<element_type_name> >
element_type_name::=  denotable_object_type_name
inverse_traversal_path_name ::=   traversal_path_name
traversal_path_name::= string_of_characters
collection_type      ::=    Set | Bag | List | Varray
```

Examples:

```
class Professor: public Pobject {
    public:
        Ref<Department>  dept
            inverse Department::professors;
        Set <Student> advisees
            inverse Student::advisor;
        }
class Student: public Pobject {
    public:
        Ref<Professor> advisor
            inverse Professor::advisees;
        Set <Course> classes
            inverse Course::students_enrolled;
        }
class Course: public Pobject {
    public:
        Set <Student> students_enrolled
            inverse Student::classes;
        }
```

5.2.3 Unidirectional Relationship Declarations

In order to accommodate a common practice in C++ programming, a degenerate form of a relationship is allowed, that which specifies a one-way path. In this case, the inverse clause is omitted.

The application is then responsible to maintain the relationship consistently when the object(s) at the end of the path is (are) deleted.

Such unidirectional relationship declarations are allowed both inside a class and inside embedded structured attributes.

Examples:

```
struct Responsible{
  char* Department;
  Ref<Employee> e;
  Date date;
};

class Order{
  public:
    Ref<Client> who;
    Set<Item> what;
    Responsible contact;
};
```

5.2.4 Operation Declarations

Operation declarations in C++ are syntactically identical to *function member* declarations, including the specification of exceptions raised.

Examples:

```
void grant_tenure ();
void assign_course (Ref<Course>);
```

5.3 C++ OML

This section describes the C++ binding for the OML. A guiding principle in the design of C++ OML is that the syntax used to create, delete, identify, reference, get/set property values, and invoke operations on a persistent object should be, so far as possible, no different than that used for objects of shorter lifetimes. A single expression may freely intermix references to persistent and transient objects.

While it is our long-term goal that nothing can be done with persistent objects that cannot also be done with transient objects, this standard treats persistent and transient objects slightly differently. Queries and transaction consistency apply only to persistent objects.

5.3.1 Object Creation, Deletion, Modification, and References

Objects can be created, deleted, and modified. Objects are created in C++ OML using the new operator, which is overloaded to accept additional arguments specifying the lifetime of the object. An optional storage pragma allows the programmer to specify how the newly allocated object is to be clustered with respect to other objects.

The formal C++ forms of the new operator are:

```
(1) void* operator new(size_t size, const char* typename =0);
(2) void* operator new(size_t size, Ref<Pobject> clustering,
                                   const char* typename=0);
(3) void* operator new(size_t size, Database& database,
                                   const char* typename=0);
```

(1) is used for creation of transient objects. (2) and (3) create persistent objects. In (2) the user specifies that the newly created object should be placed "near" the existing clustering object. The exact interpretation of "near" is implementation-defined. An example interpretation would be "on the same page if possible." In (3) the user specifies that the newly created object should be placed in the specified database, but no further clustering is specified.

The size argument, which appears as the first argument in each signature, is the size of the representation of an object. It is determined by the compiler as a function of the class of which the new object is an instance, not passed as an explicit argument by a programmer writing in the language.

The optional typename argument is used in some implementations.

Implementations must provide at least these three forms and may provide variants on these forms, with additional parameters. Each additional parameter must have a default value. This allows applications that do not use the additional parameters to be portable. Typical uses for additional parameters would be to request allocation in shared memory or to pass a string form of the class name.

Examples:

```
(1) Ref<Schedule> temp_sched1 = new Schedule;
(2) Ref<Professor> prof2 = new(yourDB,"Professor") Professor;
(3) Ref<Student> student1 = new(myDB) Student;
(4) Ref<Student> student2 = new(student1) Student;
```

Statement (1) creates a transient object temp_sched1. Statements (2)-(4) create persistent objects. Statement (2) creates a new instance of class Professor in the database yourDB. Statement (2) also illustrates passing a class name as the value of the optional third argument. Particular forms of this argument may be required by some implementations. Statement (3) creates a new instance of class Student in the database myDB. Statement (4) does the same thing, except that it specifies that the new object, student2, should be placed close to student1.

5.3.1.1 Object Deletion

Objects, once created, can be deleted in C++ OML using the Ref::destroy member function. Deleting an object is permanent. The object is removed from memory and, if it is a persistent object, from the database. The Ref instance still exists in memory but its reference value (the object to which it had referred) is set to NULL. Its Ref::is_active status is set to FALSE. An attempt to access this object from other Ref instances will fail.

Example:

```
Ref<anyType> obj_ref1;
obj_ref1.destroy();
```

The destroy operation is used in C++ OML instead of the delete operator, because C++ requires the operand of delete to be a pointer. All other C++ rules apply.

5.3.1.2 Object Modification

The state of an object is modified by updating its properties or, in some cases, running operations against it. Updates to persistent objects are made visible to other potential users of the database when the transaction containing the modifications commits.

Persistent objects that have been destroyed or modified must communicate to the runtime ODBMS process the fact that their states have changed. The ODBMS will then update the database with these new states at transaction commit time. Object change is communicated by invoking the Pobject::mark_modified member function, which is defined and used as follows:

```
void Pobject::mark_modified();
obj_ref1->mark_modified();
```

The mark_modified function call is included in the constructor and destructor methods for persistence-capable classes. The developer should also include it in any other methods that modify persistent objects.

As a convenience, the programmer may omit calls to mark_modified on objects where classes have been compiled using an optional C++ ODL preprocessor switch; the system will automatically detect when the objects are modified. In the default case, mark_modified calls are required, because in some ODMG implementations performance will be better when the programmer explicitly calls mark_modified.

5.3.1.3 Object References

Objects, whether persistent or not, may refer to other objects via object references. In C++ OML object references are instances of the templated class Ref< > (see Section 5.3.5). All accesses to persistent objects are made via methods defined on class Ref and class Pobject. The dereference operator -> is used to access members of the persistent object "addressed" by a given object reference. How an object reference converts an object's database address (its OID) to a memory address is left to the ODBMS implementor.

A dereference operation on an object reference always guarantees that the object referred to is returned or an exception is raised. The behavior of a reference is as follows. If an object (persistent or transient) refers to a second, persistent, object that is not in memory when the dereference is executed, the second object, if it exists, will be retrieved automatically from disk, mapped into memory, and returned as the result of the dereference. If the supposedly referenced object does not exist, an appropriate exception is raised. References to transient objects work exactly the same (at least on the surface) as references to persistent objects.

Any object reference may be set to the value NULL to indicate that the reference does not refer to an object.

The rules for when an object of one lifetime may refer to an object of another lifetime are a straightforward extension of the C++ rules for its two forms of transient objects — procedure coterminus and process coterminus. An object can always refer to another object of longer lifetime. An object can only refer to an object of shorter lifetime as long as the shorter lived object exists. There are two cases that require special consideration: when a persistent object is activated into memory and when a scope is terminated.

A persistent object is retrieved from disk upon activation. It is the application's responsibility to initialize the values of any of that object's references to transient objects. When a persistent object is committed, the ODBMS sets its references to transient objects to the value NULL.

In C++ when a scope is terminated, e.g. exiting a procedure, the stack frame is deleted. Any references from static or heap objects (lifetime=coterminous with process) to objects allocated within that stack frame (lifetime=procedure coterminous) become meaningless. One of the things that has made C and C++ so error-prone is that such use of pointers allows dangling references to the storage once occupied by the representation of objects that have been deleted. C++ OML gives the programmer a means to avoid dangling references. Traversal functions on relationships support bidirectional traversal and guarantee valid references. An attempt to traverse a relationship between two objects will raise an exception if the target object has been deleted.

5.3.1.4 Object Names

A database application generally will begin processing by accessing one or more critical objects and proceeding from there. These objects are in some sense "root" objects, in that they lead to interconnected webs of other objects. The ability to name an object and retrieve it later by that name facilitates this start-up capability. Named objects are also convenient in many other situations.

There is a single, flat name scope per database; thus all names in a particular database are unique. A name does not have to be defined as an attribute of an object. Object--to-name mappings for a database are stored in a directory structure, associated with that database. The operations for manipulating names are defined in the Database class in Section 5.3.8.

5.3.2 Properties

5.3.2.1 Attributes

C++ OML uses standard C++ for accessing attributes. For example, the id_number of professor Newton found above can be accessed and modified as follows:

```
prof1->id_number = get_next_id;
cout << prof1->id_number;
```

Modifying an attribute's value is considered a modification to the enclosing object instance. Mark_modified for the object must be called before the transaction commit.

The C++ binding supports embedding instances of C++ objects. However, embedded objects are not considered "independent objects" and have no object identity or OID of their own. Users are not permitted to get a Ref to an embedded object. Just as with any attribute, modifying an embedded object is considered a modification to the enclosing object instance, and mark_modified for the object must be called before the transaction commit.

5.3.2.2 Relationships

The ODL specifies which relationships exist between object classes. Creating, traversing, and breaking relationships between instances are defined in the C++ OML. Both to-one and to-many traversal paths are supported by the OML. The integrity of relationships is maintained by the ODBMS.

For any given "tPath", where tPath is a member representing a to-one traversal path of a relationship, there must exist the following methods:

```
void tPath.set (Ref<TargetClass>);
Ref<TargetClass> tPath.get(void);
boolean tPath.exists(void) const;
boolean tPath.exists(Ref<TargetClass>) const;
void tPath.delete(void);
boolean toOnePath.exists(void) const;
boolean toOnePath::exists (Ref<TargetClass>) const;
void toOnePath::delete(void);
&Ref<TargetClass> tPath::operator=(Ref<TargetClass>) const;
Ref<TargetClass> tPath();
```

The tPath in C++ ODL must be treated as a tPath attribute in C++ OML, and that attribute must, in turn, be an instance of a class that defines the set, get, exists, and delete methods. The set method creates the relationship between the object of which tPath is a member and the instance of the target class addressed by the supplied object reference. The get method returns an object reference that addresses an object that was previously set to be related, while exists checks for the existence of either the relationship in general (first version) or a relationship to a specific object (second version). Finally, delete removes the relationship.

For any given tPath, where tPath is a member representing a to-many traversal path of a relationship, there must exist the following methods:

```
void tPath.insert(Ref<TargetClass>);
void tPath.remove(Ref<TargetClass>);
Iterator<TargetClass>  tPath.create_iterator(boolean stable=FALSE);
int tPath.exists(void) const;
int tPath.exists(Ref<TargetClass>) const;
void tPath.delete(void);
```

To-many relationships use the operation insert instead of set because many target objects can be related to the current object via this single relationship. For the same reason, remove is capable of discarding only a single target object from the to-many relationship. The delete and exists methods work essentially the same as the methods for to-one relationships; note that delete removes *all* relationships defined via the given attribute from the current object to *all* target objects. An iterator is used to access each of the object references that can be reached by this traversal path.

This specification supports the concept of iterators via a general template class called Iterator, but there is certainly no reason that specialized subtemplates of that class could not be defined.

The class may also define other, vendor-specific methods, of course. But, most importantly, the class must manage any referential integrity that is required and any vendor-specific relationship characteristics that were declared in the C++ ODL.

A conforming implementation may choose to use a single "base" class for all types of relationships or it may define specialized relationship classes. In the example given above, the class would have to maintain the declared bidirectional integrity.

Examples:

```
p—>dept = english_dept;  // create 1:1 relationship
p—>dept = null;          // delete relationship
p—>advisees.insert (Sam); // add Sam to the set of students that are p's
                         // advisees; same effect as 'Sam—>advisor = p'
p—>advisees.remove(Sam); // remove Sam from the set of students that
                      // are p's advisees, and also sets to null Sam->advisor
```

The same "generator" concept applies for to-many traversal paths that applied for to-one traversal paths. In the syntax of C++ ODL, a to-many traversal path looks like an instance of a simple collection class (where each collection class is actually a class template). However, in order to implement the semantics of relationships, the traversal path must be converted to a C++ OML attribute that is an instance of a class that "understands" the type of traversal path that was declared.

5.3.3 Operations

Operations are defined in the OML as they are generally implemented in C++. Operations on transient and persistent objects behave entirely consistently with the operational context defined by standard C++. This includes all overloading, dispatching, function call structure and invocation, member function call structure and invocation, argument passing and resolution, exception handling, and compile time rules.

5.3.4 Pobject Class

A class Pobject is introduced that is defined as follows:

```
class  Pobject{
   public:
       mark_modified();            //mark Object as modified
   }
```

This class is introduced to allow the type definer to specify when a class is capable of having persistent as well as transient instances. A class A that is persistence capable would be declared as:

```
class A : Pobject {...};
```

Some implementations, although they accept the Pobject superclass as an indication of potential persistence, need not physically introduce a Pobject class. All implementations will accept the mark_modified call, but some may implement it as a no-op.

5.3.5 Ref Class

Objects may refer to other objects through a smart pointer or reference called a Ref. A Ref is a template class defined as follows:

```
template <class T> class Ref {
   public:
   Ref<T>(const T*);              //constructor
   Ref<T>(const Ref<T> &);        //constructor
   Ref<T>& operator=(const T*);//the T won't change
   Ref<T>& operator=(const Ref<T>&);//rvalue doesn't change
   T* operator->( );              //dereference the reference
```

```
        const T* operator->( );         //pointer you get back is a const
        operator T*( );                 //applies to something that is non-const
        operator const T*( );           //applies to something that is a const
        operator T*( );                 //strip away the const-ness for the reference
        boolean operator==(const Ref<T> &) const;
                                        //do these refs refer to the same object?
        boolean operator==(const T*) const;
                    //does this Ref and that pointer refer to same obj?
        boolean operator!=(const Ref<T> &) const;
                                        //do these refs refer to different objects?
        boolean operator!=(const T*) const;
                    //does this Ref and that pointer refer to diff. objects
        T& operator *( ) const;
        const T& operator *( ) const;
        T& operator[] (int);            //array behavior
        virtual ~Ref<T>;                //destructor
        boolean is_deleted( ) const;  //is object referred to by Ref deleted?
        boolean is_active( ) const;//is object referred to by Ref active (in memory)
        void destroy( );//delete the object from memory and the database
    }
```

References in many respects behave like C++ pointers but provide an additional mechanism that guarantees integrity in references to persistent objects. Although the syntax for declaring a Ref is different than for declaring a pointer, the usage is, in most cases, the same due to overloading; e.g., Refs may be dereferenced with the * operator, indexed via the [] operator, assigned with the = operator, etc. A Ref to a class may be assigned to a Ref to a superclass. Refs may be sub-classed to provide specific referencing behavior. When an object is deleted (when the destroy function is called) the Ref value is set to NULL. An application should use only these specified Ref methods and cannot depend on the implementation of the Ref class, because the implementation will vary from vendor to vendor.

The validity of a Ref after a transaction commit or abort is not guaranteed by this specification.

5.3.6 Collection Classes

The ODMG object model includes collection type generators, collection types, and collection instances. Collection type generators are represented as *template classes* in C++. Collection types are represented as collection classes, and collection instances are represented as collection instances. To illustrate these three categories, Set<T> is a collection template. Set_of_Ship is a collection class. And Cunard_Line_Ships is a particular collection, an instance of the type Set_of_Ship.

The subtype/supertype hierarchy of collection types defined in the ODMG Object Model (Section 2.6.3) is directly carried over into C++. The type Collection and its immediate subtypes, Insertion_Defined_Collection and Predicate_Defined_Collection, are abstract classes in C++. They have no direct instances. They are instantiable only through their derived classes. The only differences between the collection classes in the C++ binding and their counterparts in Section 2.6.3 are the following:

- Named operations in the Object Model are mapped to C++ function members.
- For some operations, the C++ binding includes both the named function and an overloaded infix operation, e.g., Set:: insert() also has the form operator +=. The statements s1.insert(element) and s1 += element are functionally equivalent.
- Operations that return a boolean in Section 2.6.3 are modeled as function members that return an int in the C++ binding. This is done to match a long-standing C convention that a zero-valued int = false; any other value = true.
- The create and delete operations defined in Section 2.6.3 have been replaced with C++ constructors and destructors.

Given an object type T, the declaration

```
Collection <T>    c;
```

defines a collection whose elements are of type Ref<T>. If this collection is assigned to another collection of the same type, the "copy semantics" is respected, which means that all the references are copied into the target collection. This copy is a shallow copy; i.e., the objects themselves are referenced by both collections after the assignment. This holds in any scope; in particular, if c is declared inside a class, the collection itself will be embedded inside an instance of this class. When an object of this class is copied into another object of the same class, the embedded collection is copied, too, following the copy semantics defined above. This must be differentiated from the declaration

```
Ref <Collection<T> >rc;
```

which defines a reference to a collection. When such a reference is defined as a property of a class, that means that the collection itself is an independent object which lies outside an instance of the class. Several objects may then share the same collection, since copying an object will not copy the collection, but just a reference to it. These are illustrated in Figure 5-2, below.

Collections (and all subtypes of Collection) of literals, including both atomic and structured literals, are defined as part of the standard. Collection<literal_type_name> is then defined with the same behavior; e.g., Collection<int>, Collection<struct>.

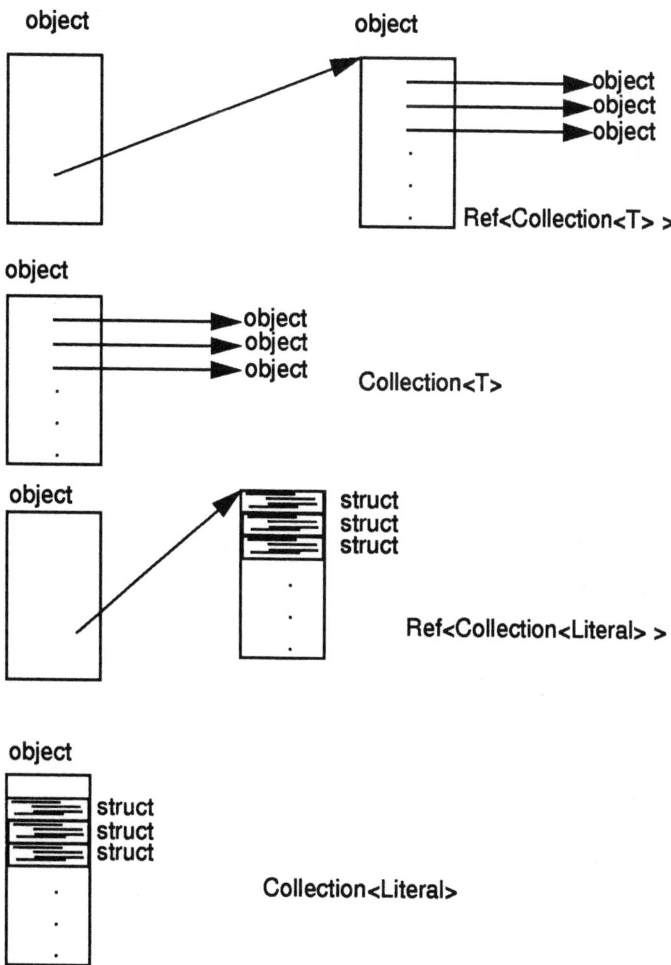

Figure 5-2. Collections, Embedded and with Ref

A conforming implementation must support at least the following subtypes of collection:

- Set
- Bag
- List
- Varray

The C++ class definitions for each of these types are defined in the subsections that follow. Indices are defined in the subsection on class Collection. Iterators are defined as a final subsection.

5.3.6.1 Class Collection

Definition:

```
template <class T> class Collection
{
   public:
      unsigned long cardinality();
      boolean empty() const;
      boolean ordered() const;
      boolean allows_duplicates() const;
      Collection ();
      ~Collection();
      boolean operator== (Ref<Collection<T> >) const;
      boolean operator!= (Ref<Collection<T> >) const;
      Collection<T>& operator= (Ref<Collection<T> >);
      Ref<Collection<T> > copy () const;             //shallow copy
      Iterator<T> create_iterator(boolean stable=FALSE);
      void insert_element (Ref<T>);
      void operator+= (Ref<T>);                      //same as insert_element
      void remove_element (Ref<T>);
      void operator-= (Ref<T>);                      //same as remove_elem
      void remove_element_at (const Iterator<T>&);
      void replace_element_at (Ref<T>,const Iterator<T>&);
      Ref<T> retrieve_element_at (const Iterator<T>&);
      Ref<T> select_element (const char *predicate);
      Iterator <T> select (const char * predicate);
      int query (Ref<Collection<T> >&, const char * fullOQL_predicate);
      boolean exists_element (const char* predicate) const;
      boolean contains_element (Ref<T>) const;
   }
```

5.3.6.2 Class Set

Definition:

```
template <class T> class Set:Collection
  {
  public:
     Set ();
     ~Set();
     int query (Ref<Set<T> >&, const char * fullOQL_predicate) const;
     Ref<Set<T> > union (const Ref<Set<T> > s2) const;
     Ref<Set<T> > operator+ (const Ref<Set<T> > s2) const;//union
     Ref<Set<T> > intersection (const Ref<Set<T> > s2) const;
     Ref<Set<T> > operator* (const Ref<Set<T> > s2) const;//intersection
     Ref<Set<T> > difference (const Ref<Set<T> > s2) const;
     Ref<Set<T> > operator- (const Ref<Set<T> > s2) const; //difference
     Ref<Set<T> > copy () const;
     boolean  is_subset_of (const Ref<Set<T> > s2) const;
     boolean  is_proper_subset_of (const  Ref<Set<T> > s2) const;
     boolean  is_superset_of (const Ref<Set<T> > s2) const;
     boolean  is_proper_superset_of (const Ref<Set<T> >s2) const;
  }
```

Note that all operations defined on type Collection are inherited by type Set, e.g., insert, remove, select_element, select, ...

Examples:

- creation:
```
Ref<Set <Professor> > my_profs = new(persistent) Set<Professor>;
```
- deletion:
```
my_profs —>delete();
```
- insertion:
```
my_prof—>insert_element (Guttag);
```
- removal:
```
my_profs—>remove_element (Guttag);
```
- iteration over members:
```
// students is a previously declared Set<Student>
Ref<Student> s;
Iterator <Student> iter = students.create_iterator();
while ( iter.next(s))
   {
      ...
```

```
        }
    iter.close();
```

5.3.6.3 Class Bag

Definition:

```
template <class T> class Bag:Collection
   {
   public:
      Bag();
      ~Bag();
      int query(Ref<Bag<T> >&,  const char *predicate) const;
      Ref<Bag<T> > union (const Ref<Bag<T> > b2) const;
      Ref<Bag<T> > operator+ (const Ref<Bag<T> > b2) const;
      Ref<Bag<T> > intersection (const Ref<Bag<T> > b2) const;
      Ref<Bag<T> > operator* (const Ref<Bag<T> > b2) const;
      Ref<Bag<T> > difference (const Ref<Bag<T> > b2) const;
      Ref<Bag<T> > operator- (const Ref<Bag<T> > b2) const;
}
```

5.3.6.4 Class List

Definition:

```
template <class T> class List:Collection
   {
   public:
      List ();
      ~List();
      Ref<T> operator[] (int);
      Ref<T> retrieve_element_at (int position); //same as []
      void replace_element_at (Ref<T> element, int position);
      Ref<List<T> > concat(Ref<List<T> >);
      Ref<List<T> > operator+(Ref<List<T> >);
      void append (Ref<List<T> >);
      void operator+= (Ref<List<T> >);
      int query (Ref<List<T> >&, char * fullOQL_predicate);
      void insert_element_after ( Ref<T> element, int position);
      void insert_element_before (Ref<T> element, int position);
      void insert_element_first (Ref<T> element);
      void insert_element_last (Ref<T> element);
      void remove_element_at (int position);
      void remove_first_element ();
```

```
        void remove_last_element();
        Ref<T> retrieve_first_element ();
        Ref<T> retrieve_last_element ();
        int find_element (Ref<T>);//returns index, -1 if not found
};
```

5.3.6.5 Class Array

The Array type defined in Section 2.3.1 is implemented by the built-in array defined by the C++ language. This is a single dimension, fixed-length array.

5.3.6.6 Class Varray

Definition:

```
template <class T> class Varray:Collection
{
public:
    Varray (int length);
    ~Varray();
    Ref<T> operator[] (int);
    int query (Ref<Varray<T> >&,  const char * fullOQL_predicate);
    void remove_element_at (int position);
    void replace_element_at (Ref<T> element, int position);
    Ref<T> retrieve_element_at (int position);
    void resize(int length);
    int find_element (Ref<T>); //returns index, -1 if not found
    int upper_bound() const;
};
```

Examples:

```
Varray<double>  vector[1000];
vector.replace_element_at[97] = 3.14159;
vector.resize[2000];
```

5.3.6.7 Class Iterator

A template class, Iterator <T>, defines the generic behavior for iteration. All iterators use a consistent protocol for sequentially returning each element from the collection over which the iteration is defined. The type parameter supplied may be any concrete subclass of Collection. A template class has been used to give us type-safe iterators, i.e., iterators that are guaranteed to return an instance of the type of the element of the collection over which the iterator is defined. Iterators are stable with respect to iteration as specified in Section 2.6.2. Normally, an iterator is initialized by the method create_iterator() on a collection class. Close returns the iterator to uninitialized state. It's destructor must automatically do a close().

The template class Iterator<T> is defined as follows:

```
template <class T> class Iterator
   {
   public:
       Iterator();
       ~Iterator();
       reset();      //resets iterator to beginning of collection
       boolean next (Ref<T> &);
       close ();
   }
```

The function member next() has been defined to return, as an argument, a reference to a member of the collection over which the iterator is defined. It also returns a boolean value, which will be true if an element is returned; false if there are no more elements to return. Specifically, on the last element it returns true, but the call following this will return false and the value of the argument is undefined. Thus, the test for the end of the iteration can be made without introducing an additional function member call on each pass through a loop iterating over the members of the collection. See statement (2) in the example below.

Example:

Given the class Student, with extent students:

```
(1) Iterator<Student> it = students.create_iterator();
    Ref<Student> s;
(2) while (it.next(s))
    {
        ....
    }
```

Statement (1) defines an iterator it that ranges over the collection students. Statement (2) iterates through this collection, returning one student on each successive call and binding it to the loop variable s. The body of the while statement is then executed once for each student in the collection students.

5.3.7 Transactions

Transaction semantics are defined in the object model explained in Chapter 2.

A default lock is specified as an implicit part of the concurrency model. It indicates the kind of lock that will be aquired by default by any object activated into memory during a transaction. The default lock is a read_lock lock.

Transactions can be started, committed, aborted, and checkpointed. Transactions must be explicitly started. Transactions may be nested. It is important to note that *all access, creation, modification, and deletion of persistent objects must be done within a transaction.*

Transactions are implemented in C++ as objects of class Transaction. The class Transaction defines the operation for starting, committing, aborting, and checkpointing transactions. These operations are:

```
enum lock_type {read_lock, write_lock, default_lock};
class Transaction {
   Transaction( );
   ~Transaction( );
   void start( );
   void commit( );
   void abort( );
   void checkpoint( );
};
```

Transactions must be explicitly created and started; they are not automatically started on database open or following a transaction commit or abort.

Creating a transaction object does exactly and only that. It does not start the transaction.

Start() starts a transaction, and must be explicitly called. Calling start multiple times on the same transaction object, without an intervening commit or abort, raises an exception on the second and subsequent calls.

Calling commit commits all persistent objects to the database and releases locks. It does not delete the transaction object.

Calling checkpoint commits the objects to the database and retains the locks on these objects. Any mark_modified flags are cleared.

Calling abort aborts changes to objects and releases the locks, and does not delete the transaction object.

The destructor aborts the transaction if it is active, and obviously deletes the object.

In the current standard, transient objects are not subject to transaction semantics. Committing a transaction does not remove transient objects from memory. Aborting a transaction does not restore the state of modified transient objects.

Transaction objects are not long-lived (beyond process boundaries) and cannot be stored to the database. This means that transaction objects may not be made persistent and that the notion of "long transactions" is not defined in this specification.

Deleting (destroying) a transaction object aborts the transaction.

Transactions may be nested. The commit of inner transactions is only relative to the outermost transaction; the changes made in an inner transaction only commit if all of its containing outer transactions also commit. If an inner transaction commits and the outer transaction aborts, the changes made in the inner transaction are aborted as well.

Unless explicitly specified, objects activated into memory are locked with the default lock for the active concurrency control policy. Some member functions, such as lookup and Iterators, support explicit specification of the lock type.

In summary the rules that apply to object modification (necessarily, during a transaction) are:

1. Changes made to persistent objects within a transaction can be "undone" by aborting the transaction.
2. Transient objects are standard C++ objects.
3. Persistent objects created within the scope of a transaction are handled consistently at transaction boundaries: stored to the database and removed from memory (at transaction commit) or deleted (as a result of a transaction abort).

5.3.8 Database Operations

There is a predefined type Database. It supports the following methods:

```
enum AccessStatus {NotOpen, ReadWrite, ReadOnly, Exclusive};
class Database {
   public:
   open (const char* database_name, AccessStatus status = ReadWrite);
   close ();
   delete ()
   void name (const Ref<Pobject> theObject, const char* theName);
   const char* name (Ref<Pobject> theObject);
   void rename (const char* oldName, const char* newName);
   void lookup (const Ref<Pobject> & o, const char* name,
                 lock_type lock = default_lock);
}
```

The database object, like the transaction object, is transient. Databases cannot be created programmatically using C++ OML. Databases must be opened before starting any transactions which use the database, and closed after committing (or aborting) these transactions.

To open a database, use the method open, defined on class Database, which takes the name of the database as its argument. This initializes the instance of the Database object.

```
database—>open ("myDB");
```

This method locates the named database and makes the appropriate connection to the database. For example:

```
database—>open ("myDB");
```

You must open a database before you can access objects in that database. Extensions to the open method will enable some ODBMSs to implement default database names and/or implicitly open a default database when a database session is started. Some ODBMSs may support opening logical as well as physical databases. Some ODBMSs may support being connected to multiple databases at the same time.

To close a database, use the method close, defined on class Database:

```
database—>close();
```

This method does appropriate clean-up on the named database connection.

Example:

```
database—>close();
```

After you have closed a database, further attempts to access objects in the database will be rejected. This specification does not prescribe the behavior at program termination if databases are not closed or transactions not committed or aborted; some ODBMSs may default to closing open databases and terminating (committing or aborting) current transactions.

The name methods allow manipulating names of objects. The first form of the name function assigns a character string name to the object referenced. If the string supplied as the name argument is not unique within the database, a NameInUse exception is raised. If the object already has a name, it is renamed to the new name. The second form of the name function returns the name of the specified object. The rename method changes the name of an object. If the new name is already in use, a NameInUse exception is raised and the old name is retained. A named object may have its name removed by providing NULL as a value for the new name. When a named object is deleted, its entry is automatically removed from the directory.

An object is accessed by name using the Database::lookup member function:

```
void lookup (Ref<Pobject>& o, const char* name,
             lock_type lock = default_lock);
```

At runtime the type of the first parameter is checked against the type of the object found by the lookup. If it does not match, an exception is raised.

Example:

```
Ref<Professor> prof;
myDatabase->lookup(prof, "Newton");
```

The explicit cast is necessary. The object named Newton is retrieved, and a valid reference is placed into prof1. If no such object exists, then NULL is returned.

5.4 C++ OQL

Chapter 4 outlined the Object Query Language. In this section the OQL semantics are mapped into the C++ language. There are generally two options for binding a query sublanguage to a programming language: loosely coupled or tightly coupled. In the loosely coupled approach query functions are introduced that take strings containing queries as their arguments. These functions parse and evaluate the query at runtime, returning the result as the result of the function, result. In the tightly coupled approach the query sublanguage is integrated directly into the programming language by expanding the definition of the nonterminals <term>, <expression> as defined in the BNF of the programming language. The tightly coupled approach allows queries to be optimized at compile time; in the loosely coupled approach they are generally optimized at execution time. The C++ binding for OQL supports two variants of the loosely coupled approach:

- a query method defined on the generic class Collection
- a free-standing oql function not bound to any class

The two variants are defined in the subsections which follow.

5.4.1 Query Method on Class Collection

Each collection class comes with a query function member whose signature is:

```
int query(Ref<Collection<T> >& result, const char* predicate);
```

This function filters the collection using the predicate and assigns the result to the first parameter. It returns a code different from 0, if the query is not well formed.
The predicate is given as a string with the syntax of the *where* clause of OQL. The predefined variable this is used inside the predicate to denote the current element of the collection to be filtered.

Example:

Given the class **Student**, as defined in Chapter 3, with extent **Students**, compute the set of students who take math courses:

```
Ref<Set<Student> > mathematicians;
Students->query(mathematicians,
            "exists s in this.takes: s.section_of.name = \"math\" ");
```

5.4.2 OQL Function

The oql function allows the programmer to gain access to the whole functionality of OQL from a C++ program. It is a free-standing function, not part of any class definition. It takes as parameters a reference to a variable to store the result, the OQL sentence, and a variable length list of C++ expressions whose values are input operands for the query. Inside the query these operands are identified with the syntax given below. The function returns a code different from 0 if the query is not well formed.

The signatures of this overloaded function are:

- A query returning an object.
  `int oql(Ref<Pobject>& result, const char* query, ...)`
- A query returning a collection.
  `int oql(Collection& result, const char* query, ...)`
- A query returning an atom.
  `int oql(int&, const char* query, ...)`
  `int oql(char&, const char* query, ...)`
  `int oql(double&, const char* query, ...)`
- A query returning a string. In this case, the result is dynamically allocated by OQL. The program is responsible for deallocating the string when no longer used.
  `int oql(char*&, const char* query, ...)`

Beside the two first parameters, oql accepts an optional list of runtime parameters. Each of these parameters is valued with any C++ expression. The query sentence refers to the i-th parameter of this list through a binding notation whose syntax is:

```
$<range><type>
```

<range> is an integer which gives the rank of the parameter (starting from 1).

<type> is a character which defines the type of the C++ expression:

- i denotes an integer (int)
- c denotes a character (char)
- r denotes a real (double)
- s denotes a string (char*)

- k denotes a collection (object from a Collection<T> subclass)
- o denotes an object (object from a Ref<T> subclass)

Type checking of the input parameters according their use in the query is done at run-time. Similarly the type of the result of the query is checked to match the type of the first parameter. Any violation of type would raise an exception.

If the query returns a mutable object, it is directly assigned to the result variable which must be a Ref variable. If the query returns a structured literal, the value of it is assigned to the value of the object or collection denoted by the result variable, provided that types match.

Example:

Among the math students (computed before as in Section 5.4.2 into the variable mathematicians) who are teaching assistants and earn more than x, find the set of professors that they assist. We suppose there exists an extent for teaching assistants which is called TA.

```
Set<Student> mathematicians; // computed as above
Set<Professor> assisted_profs;
double x = ...

oql(assisted_profs, "select t.assists.taught_by \
                    from t in TA where t.salary > $1r and t in $2k",
                    x, mathematicians);
```

5.5 Example

This section gives a complete example of a small C++ application. This application manages people records. A Person may be entered into the database. Then special events can be recorded: his/her marriage, the birth of children, his/her moving to a new address.

The application comprises two transactions: the first one populates the database, while the second consults and updates it.

The next section defines the schema of the database, as C++ ODL classes. The C++ program is given in the subsequent section.

5.5.1 Schema Definition

For the explanation of the semantics of this example, see Section 3.4 Another ODL Example. Here is the C++ ODL syntax:

```
// Schema Definition in C++ ODL
    class City;                     // forward declaration

    struct Address{
        int number;
        char* street;
        Ref<City> city;             // reference to a City Object

        Address(int, const char*, Ref<City>);  // constructs Address structure
        Address(const Address&);          // copies an Address structure
    };

    class Person : Pobject{
    public:
    // Attributes (all public, for this example)
        char* name;
        Address address;
    // Relationships
        Ref<Person> spouse inverse spouse;
        List<Person> children inverse parents;
        Ref<Person> parents[2] inverse children;[1]
    // Operations
        Person(const char* name);// constructs a new Person Object
        void birth(Ref<Person> child);              // a new child is born
        void marriage(Ref<Person> with);            // a spouse for this Person
        Ref<Set<Person> > ancestors();// returns the ancestors of this Person
        void move(Address);        // moves this Person to a new Address
    // Extension
        static Ref<Set<Person> >  people;
                                    // a reference to the class extension[2]
    };

    class City : Pobject {
    public:
    // Attributes
        int city_code;
```

1. As specified in the class Array section, we use the standard C++ syntax for this relationship.

2. This (transient) static variable will be initialized at transaction begin time (see the application program, below).

```
        char* name;
        Ref<Set<Person> > population;           // the people living in this
City
    // Operations
        City(int, const char*)                  // constructs a new City
Object
    // Extension
        static Ref<Set<Cityy> >  cities; // a reference to the class extension3
    };
```

5.5.2 Schema Implementation

We now define the code of the operations declared in the schema. This is written in plain C++. We assume that the C++ ODL preprocessor has generated a file which is called "schema.hxx" and which contains the standard C++ definitions equivalent to the C++ ODL classes.

```
// Classes Implementation in C++
#include "schema.hxx"
#include <string.h>

// Address Structure:

    Address::Address(int number, const char* street, Ref<City> city){
    // Constructs an Address
        this->number = number;
        this->street = new char[strlen(street)+1];
        strcpy(this->street, street);
    }

    Address::Address(const Address& copy){
    // Copies an Address
        number = copy.number;
        city = copy.city;
        street = new char[strlen(copy.street) +1];
        strcpy(street, copy.street);
    }

// Person Class:
```

---

3. See Section 2.

```
Person::Person(const char* name):address(0,0,0⁴){
// Constructs a Person, with the attribute address initialized to none.
    this->name = new char[strlen(name)+1];
    strcpy(this->name, name);
    people->insert_element(this);
            // Put this Person in the extension
}

void Person::birth(Ref<Person> child){
// Adds a new child to the children list
    children.insert_element_last(child);
    if(spouse != 0⁵)
        spouse->children.insert_element_last(child);
}
void Person::marriage(Ref<Person> with){
// Initializes the spouse relationship
    spouse = with;
    // with->spouse is automatically set to be equal to this Person
}

Ref<Set<Person> > Person::ancestors(){
// Constructs the set of all ancestors of this Person
    Ref<Set<Person> > the_ancestors = new Set<Person>;
    int i;
    for(i = 0; i < 2; i++)
        if(parents[i]⁶ != 0⁷){
            // The ancestors = parents union ancestors(parents)
            the_ancestors->insert_element(parents[i]);
            Ref<Set<Person> > grand_parents = parents[i]->ancestors();
            the_ancestors = the_ancestors->union(grand_parents);
            grand_parents.destroy();
        }
    return the_ancestors;
```

[4] Notice that the last '0' is converted automatically to Ref<City>. In fact, 0 is converted to City* which is in turn converted to Ref<City>, thanks the explicit constructor defined in the Ref class.

[5] Same remark as in the previous note. 0 means the nil object of type Ref<Person>.

[6] Since the relationship is a (C++) array (see note 1), we access it as a standard C++ array. One can do that for reading it, but not for updating it, in which case the syntax would be: parents.replace_element_at(0,i).

[7] See footnote 5.

```
    }

void Person::move(Address new_address){
    // Updates the address attribute of this Person
        if(address.city != 0⁸){
            address.city->population->remove_element(this);}
        new_address.city->population->insert_element(this);
        address = new_address;
        mark_modified();⁹
    }

// City class:

    City::City(int code, const char* name){
    // Constructs a City Object
        city_code = code;
        this->name = new char[strlen(name)+1];
        strcpy(this->name, name);
        cities->insert_element(this); // Put this City into the extension
    }
```

5.5.3 An Application

We now have the whole schema well defined and implemented. We are able to populate the database and play with it. In the following application, the transaction Load builds some objects into the database. Then the transaction Consult reads it, prints some reports from it, and makes updates. Each transaction is implemented inside a C++ function.

The database is previously opened by the main program, which then starts the transactions.

```
// An Application in C++
#include "schema.hxx"
#include <stdio.h>
static Database database; //global variable seen by both transactions

void Load(){
```

---

8. See footnote 4.

9. Do not forget it! Notice that it is necessary only in the case where an attribute of the object is modified. When a relationship is updated, the object is automatically marked modified.

```
// Transaction which populates the database
Transaction load;
   load.start();

   // Create both Persons and Cities extensions, and name them.

   Person::people = new(database) Set<Person>;
   City::cities = new(database) Set<City>;

   database->name(Person::people, "people");
   database->name(City::cities, "cities");

   // Construct 3 persistent objects from class Person.

   Ref<Person> God, Adam, Eve;

   God = new(database) Person("God");
   Adam = new(database) Person("Adam");
   Eve = new(database) Person("Eve");

   // Construct an Address structure, Paradise, as (7 Apple street, Garden)
   // and set the address attributes of Adam and Eve.

   Address Paradise(7, "Apple", new(database) City(0, "Garden"));

   Adam->move(Paradise);
   Eve->move(Paradise);

   // Define the family relationships.

   God->birth(Adam);
   Adam->marriage(Eve);
   Adam->birth(new(database) Person("Cain"));
   Adam->birth(new(database) Person("Abel"));

// Commit the transaction, thus putting these objects into the database.
load.commit();
}

static void print_persons(Set<Person>& s){
// A service function to print a set of Persons
```

```
    Ref<Person> p;
    Iterator<Person> it = s.create_iterator();
    while(it.next(p)){
        printf("--- %s lives in %s\n",
            p->name,
            (p->address.city != 0) ? p->address.city->name: "unknown" );
    }
    it.close();
}

void Consult(){
// Transaction which consults and updates the database
Transaction consult;
    consult.start();
    // Static references to objects or collections must be recomputed
    // after a commit

    database->lookup(Person::people, "people");
    database->lookup(City::cities, "cities");

    // Now begin the transaction

    printf("All the people ....:\n");
    print_persons(Person::people);

    printf("All the people sorted by name ....:\n");
    oql(s, "sort p in people by p.name");
    print_persons(s);

    printf("People having 2 children and living in Paradise ...:\n");
    oql(s, "select p from p in people\
            where p.address.city != nil and p.address.city.name = \"Garden\"\
                and count(p.children) = 2");
    print_persons(s);

    // Adam and Eve are moving ...
    Address Earth(13, "Macadam", new(persistent) City(1, "St-Croix"));
    Ref<Person> Adam;
    oql(Adam, "element(select p from p in people where p.name = \"Adam\"")");
    Adam->move(Earth);
    Adam->spouse->move(Earth);
```

```
        printf("Abel's ancestors ...:\n");
        Ref<Person> Abel = Adam->children.retrieve_element_at(0);
        print_persons(Abel->ancestors());
    consult.commit();
    }

    main(){
    // Main program
        database->open("family");
        Load();
        Consult();
        database->close();
    }
```

5.6 Future Binding

This section defines the C++ ODL/OML binding we plan to offer in the future when it is practical to do so. We expect that either C++ technology will evolve to support the degree of transparency described in this section, as suggested in Appendix C, or that a C++ preprocessor can be introduced to achieve this transparency.

Stated simply, the future binding is a more complete realization of the principal that there should be no difference in the way the C++ programmer treats persistent and transient objects. At the same time, it demands a more complex implementation. In the absence of the C++ changes discussed in Section 5.6.2 and Appendix C, the future binding requires a preprocessor capable of handling the full C++ language, as well as careful integration with the major debuggers and programming environments for C++ in addition to the ODBMS runtime. In recognition of the practical difficulties of achieving robust implementations of this binding in product releases currently committed for 1993, the member companies of the ODMG have chosen to target the binding outlined in Section 5.2 to Section 5.5 as the base-line standard for intersystem application portability today, rather than the binding outlined in this Section 5.6. The future binding is defined in this standard, however, in order to anticipate a problem we — eight vendors with customer bases committed to eight different bindings, some broadly similar, others very different—had in reaching agreement on the current binding. By defining the future binding now, in advance of divergent implementations by different vendors, we preclude this problem.

The major differences between the current and future binding are in two areas: how they handle references to objects, and how the query language is integrated into the programming language.

With regard to the first of these, the current binding introduces a new reference form (Ref<T>) for classes capable of supporting persistent as well as transient instances. These classes are referred to as "persistence-capable classes" in Section 5.2 to Section 5.5 to distinguish them from "C++ classes." Support for the principle that persistence is orthogonal to type is limited, in the current binding, to these persistence-capable classes. A different syntax is used to refer to instances of the persistence-capable classes from that used to refer to instances of other C++ classes.

The future binding, by contrast, allows any C++ class to have both persistent and transient instances and allows the programmer to use the same pointer and C++ reference syntax that have always been used to refer to persistent instances of the class as well as transient instances, e.g.,

```
Professor *p;
  p->office_extension = "432"
```

in addition to

```
Ref<Professor> profpref;
  profpref->office_extension = "432"
```

This is what we mean when we say that the future binding is essentially a more complete realization of the language design principles articulated in Section 5.1 as the base for both bindings.

The second major area in which the future binding differs from the current binding is in its handling of the query sublanguage. The future binding again achieves more complete integration with C++, but again at the expense of requiring a more sophisticated implementation from the ODBMS vendor. In the current binding a programmer invokes a query function and passes the text of the query as a string to that function (see Section 5.4). The binding of programming language variables to variables in the query string is done as it is in the printf function: $1 is embedded in the query string and bound to the values of arguments passed after the query string. The binding of arguments to query variables is by position, e.g., $2i is bound to the value of the second argument; and the arguments are optional, so that queries without them or with fewer of them will not require dummy arguments. It is up to the programmer to see that the types of the arguments passed match those expected by the query variables. Results of the query are returned either as a set or through an iterator. Although the language allows arbitrary program-defined functions to be invoked within the body of the query, it will require a fairly sophisticated runtime QL interpreter to locate, bind, and execute the methods that implement these functions. We expect that many systems may restrict this capability.

The future binding, by contrast, does not require the query to be passed as a string to a function; instead it extends the definition of expressions in the grammar of the base programming language to support identification of objects by descriptions as well as by variable names. These descriptions are in the form of predicates defined on the attributes of objects, on their relationships to other objects, and on the results of operations applied to objects. This means that C++ expressions can be used freely within the query sublanguage, and expressions of the query language can be embedded as subexpressions within normal C++ expressions. There is no need for a printf-style argument binding process, and the query expression can be optimized at compile time of the program, rather than runtime.

Note that in contrast to the futures section of Chapter 2, which defined future capabilities of the Object Model (section 2.10), the future C++ binding is only a simplification of the language binding for the functionality currently defined in ODMG-93. Enhancing the standard to include more advanced functionality (and if necessary, syntax to support that advanced functionality) will be the subject of future revisions of the ODMG standard.

The body of this Section 5.6 discusses the delta between the current C++ binding and the future C++ binding. A summary list of the differences is as follows:

- All classes can have persistent instances. It is not necessary to specially designate a set of persistence-capable classes.
- Standard C++ pointers and references can be used to refer to persistent objects; a new reference type need not be introduced.
- The syntax for creating and deleting objects is fully consistent with C++: (1) automatic allocation of objects on entry to the scope of their declaration for persistent objects is supported for persistent objects as well as explicit program-requested allocation (new), and (2) the standard C++ delete() function can be used for both persistent and transient objects, a separate form for persistent objects referred to with the Ref<T> syntax is not required.
- Queries can be more smoothly integrated into the programming language.

The first three items in this list are discussed in Section 5.6.1 (ODL). The last two are discussed in Section 5.6.2 (OML). To help distinguish the ODL and OML components of the future binding from their counterparts in the current binding, the former are often referred to as ODL/future and OML/future in the body of this section.

5.6.1 ODL

The only difference between the extended C++ class declarations accepted by the ODL preprocessor of the current binding and the ODL/OML preprocessor for the future binding is in its use of standard C++ pointer syntax (*) rather than the reference type Ref<T> introduced by the current binding.

Figure 5-3 shows the ODL/future version of the class definition shown in Figure 5-1 for the current binding. As in the earlier figure, new keywords not defined by C++ are shown in bold; new keywords introducing optional clauses are shown in italics.

```
class Professor
{
    public:
        // properties:
            int age;
            char * name;
            Department * dept
                inverse Department::professors;
            Set<Student *> advisees
                inverse Student::advisor
                ordered_by student_id;
        // operations:
            void  grant_tenure ();
            void  assign_course (Course *)
                raises (course_already_covered);
    private:
        ...
}
```

Figure 5-3. C++ Class Declaration in Future Binding

Attribute declarations are the same in the current and future bindings.

Relationship declarations differ only in the use of standard C++ pointers rather than Ref<T> syntax, e.g.,

```
class Professor {
    public:
        Department * dept  inverse Department::professors;
        Set <Student *> advisees  inverse Student::advisor;
        ...
        };
```

rather than

```
class Professor {
    public:
        Ref<Department> dept_ref  inverse Department::professors;
        Set <Student> advisees  inverse Student::advisor;
        ...
        };
```

Operation signatures differ only in that the future binding uses the standard C++ pointer-to-object (*) and C++ reference-to-object (&) syntax. There is no need to use the Ref<T> form of reference to "database objects."

5.6.2 OML

The C++ OML/future is not principally a set of new expressions or statements (or even new reference forms) added to C++. It leaves unchanged the existing syntactic forms but expands their interpretation. This represents an important departure from the programming language bindings available in the relational era and from that of OML/current as well. Rather than introducing a separate sublanguage to deal with persistent data, the C++ OML expands the interpretation of the existing syntactic forms so that they can be uniformly applied to persistent as well as transient data. The C++ programming language already has objects of two lifetimes: those that live for the lifetime of the procedure in which they were first created and (2) those that live for the lifetime of the process. These differences in lifetime are implicit in two different syntactic forms used to create the objects: a declarative form for those that live for the lifetime of a procedure and an explicit function call (new) for those that outlive the procedure. Once objects of these two lifetimes have been created, however, the syntax used for manipulating them is the same. The ODBMS binding defined by the C++ OML simply adds a third lifetime for objects — persistent. A persistent object is one that outlives the process in which it was created. It lives for the lifetime of the database in which it is stored. Once a persistent object has been created, the OML/future binding allows it to be referenced and manipulated using the same syntax that C++ uses for objects of shorter lifetimes.

The OML/future binding involves only:

1. Upward compatible extensions to the C++ object creation syntax. The extensions allow the programmer to specify a third lifetime (persistent) in addition to the two already supported by the programming language.
2. Upward compatible extensions to the C++ expression syntax for referring to objects. The extensions allow selection of objects based on descriptions of those objects and the relationships they participate in (queries) rather than only on the names of the variables to which they have been assigned.

The binding continues to use the two sets of built-in classes defined by the current binding:

1. A built-in set of collection classes to support the query capability
2. A built-in set of transaction and database classes that support the controlled sharing, integrity, and recovery guarantees of the DBMS

The set of function members exported by these built-in classes is invoked using the standard C++ syntax. The only syntax extensions, then, are those related to persistent object creation and query expressions.

The details of these syntax extensions and their differences from the corresponding features of the current OML binding are outlined in the subsections that follow.

5.6.2.1 Object Creation, Deletion, and References

C++ supports implicit creation of objects when the thread of control enters the scope of a declaration, as well as explicit, programmer-controlled creation and deletion of objects using the operator **new()** and operator **delete()** funtctions. The current OML binding supports only explicit creation of persistent objects. The future binding supports both implicit and explicit creation of persistent objects.

Object Creation

Creation of persistent objects is done in the current binding by overloading the **new()** operator to accept additional arguments specifying the lifetime of the object being created and whether its state is to be kept transaction-consistent. An optional storage pragma allows the programmer to specify how the newly allocated object is to be clustered with respect to other objects on secondary storage. The syntactic form of this declaration is carried over directly into the OML/future binding, except that the **new()** call returns a C++ pointer to the newly created object in all cases, regardless of the lifetime of the object.

Syntax:

```
class_name * pointer_name =
   new (persistent [object] [,database] ) object_class_name
      [new-initializer]
```

Examples:

```
Student *s1 = new(persistent) Student;
Student *s2 = new(persistent, s1) Student;
Student *s3 = new(persistent, s1, enrollment_db) Student;
```

Object Deletion

The OML/future binding retains the C++ model of explicit object deletion. The addition of implicitly created persistent objects requires no new syntax. The standard C++ rule is that implicitly created objects are deleted on exit from the scope in which they were created. Implicitly created persistent objects are deemed to exist in a containing scope outer to those defined by the process in the course of its execution. They are therefore not deleted on process exit. If they are to be deleted, they must be explicitly deleted, just like explicitly created persistent objects.

The only difference between object deletion in the OML/current binding and the OML/future binding is in the syntax for explicit deletion. C++ defines a **delete()** operation that is used for objects allocated out of the heap. This function requires a

void* as its argument and therefore cannot be used by the OML/current binding. The current binding therefore defines a separate function, **destroy()**, to handle deletion of persistent objects. Since the OML/future binding uses standard C++ pointers to reference persistent objects as well as transient objects, there is no need for the additional **destroy()** function in the future binding. The OML/future binding simply uses the standard C++ **delete()** function for all explicitly created objects, irrespective of their lifetime.

Object Reference

In OML/future objects refer to other objects using standard C++ pointers (*) or standard C++ references (&). These forms may be used to refer to either transient or persistent objects. Pointers may be set to the value null to indicate that they do not refer to an object. Null is defined as 0 in C++.

This means that standard C++ syntax can be used for getting and setting the value of attributes, for creating, deleting, and traversing relationships, and for invoking operations; e.g.,

Examples of attribute value assignment:

```
p.age = 32;
x = p.age;
```

The first statement assigns the value 32 to the age attribute of p. The second statement assigns the value of p's age attribute to the variable x.

Examples of relationship creation, deletion, and traversal:

Given the definitions:

```
Department *english_dept;
Student *Sam;
Professor *p;
```

and the class **Professor** shown in Section 5-2,

```
p—>dept = english_dept;
p—>dept = null;
p—>advisees.insert (Sam);
p—>advisees.remove(Sam);
p—>advisees += Sam;
p—>advisees -= Sam;
Sam —> advisor = p;
```

The first of these statements creates a one-to-one relationship between the professor denoted by p and the English department. The second statement deletes that relationship. The third statement adds Sam to the set of students that are p's advisees. The fourth statement removes Sam from the set of students that are p's advisees. The next two statements use the operator += and operator -= defined on type Set to insert and remove Sam from the set of p's advisees. The last statement has the same result as the third and fifth statements — namely to create a new relationship between the student Sam and the professor p. The only difference is that it uses a statement that would be appropriate from the vantage point of someone looking at the database from the student's perspective.

Example operation invocation:

```
s.register_for (c);
```

5.6.2.2 Queries

The basic form of integrated query is:

collection|object = collection [predicate]

The expression on the right-hand side of this statement selects from the collection those elements that satisfy the predicate.

Predicates may be defined on attributes, relationships or operations.

Predicates may include a single term or a boolean conjunction of terms, e.g.,

```
Professor x;
Set <Professor*> ee_professors;
x = professors [name=="Guttag"];
ee_professors = professors {dept==electrical_engineering};
```

Brackets, for example in professors[name=="Guttag"], are used to indicate that the query subexpression should return a single object. Braces, for example in professors{dept==electrical_engineering}, are used to indicate that the query subexpression should return a set of objects.

Queries may also traverse relationships between objects, e.g.,

```
Set<Student*> guttags_students;
guttags_students = students{take Course[taught_by Professor
                                [name=="Guttag"]]};
```

This query returns the set of students who take a course taught by a professor whose name is Guttag.

The predicate syntax used in the examples of this section represents a restricted use of the full OQL syntax defined in Section 5.4. Others restrictions are possible, as is supporting the full syntax. This is the one area of the future binding in which we expect to allow the market to help us make a choice by the time the OML/future binding becomes the principal one for C++. The basic question is whether an extended

SQL-like syntax or something more akin to the structured English shown in the examples of this subsection will win.

Queries are not limited to persistent objects; they work equally well with transient objects.

5.6.2.3 Collection Operations

The collection types defined in the current binding are carried over directly into the future binding. The only difference is that arguments to functions and instances of the classes returned as the results of operations are uniformly referred to using C++ pointers and C++ references in the OML/future binding. The semantics of all functions defined on these classes remains the same and is therefore not repeated here. We show here one sample class declaration, that for the class Set, so that the programmer using the future binding will have an example of the complete operation signatures using the pointer syntax.

```
template <class T> class Set:Collection
  {
  public:
      Set ();
      ~Set();
      Set<T> union (const Set<T> *s2) const;
      Set<T> intersection (const Set<T> *s2) const;
      Set<T*> difference (const Set<T> *s2) const;
      Set<T>* copy () const;
      int is_subset_of (const Set<T> *s2) const;
      int is_proper_subset_of (const  Set<T> *s2) const;
      int is_superset_of (const Set<T> *s2) const;
      int is_proper_superset_of (const Set<T> *s2) const;
  };
```

5.6.2.4 Transaction and Database Operations

Transactions and databases are modeled as built-in classes in the future OML binding, just as they are in the current OML binding. The syntax for referring to instances of these built-in types is also the same in both bindings, since neither transactions nor the "channel" objects used to represent the connection between a process and a database are persistent objects. In the current version of the Object Model, both transient and channel objects are transient and are therefore referred to using C++ pointers in the current OML binding as well as the future binding.

5.6.3 Migration Issues

There are two paths to the future binding: (1) evolve the definition of operator overloading within the C++ language definition; (2) introduce a preprocessor that can handle C++ method bodies as well as C++ class declarations.

The preprocess, compile, and link steps required for a preprocessor implementation of the future C++ binding are shown in Figure 5-4. The diagram has been structured so that it can be directly compared with the analogous figure for the current binding, Figure 5-1. The only difference is that the preprocessor for the current binding looks at only the C++ class declarations. The preprocessor for the future binding looks at the body of the methods that implement the function members defined on the classes as well. Or, in the language of the two figures, the current binding requires an "ODL preprocessor;" the future binding requires an "ODL/OML preprocessor."

The reason the preprocessor for the future binding has to look at method bodies is that statements in these methods refer to persistent objects using the same pointer operators used to refer to transient objects always present in virtual memory. These references have to be replaced with function calls on a reference type that can determine whether or not the object referred to is already in virtual memory or not. If the object is transient, the answer will always be yes. If the object is persistent, the answer may be yes or no. If no, then an operation has to be called that makes the object present in virtual memory before completing the dereference. The second reason for needing the preprocessor is to allow the close integration of the query language with the base programming language.

A large subset of this binding— everything except the integration of query expressions with C++ expressions — can be done with either (1) an ODL-only preprocessor (like that contemplated by the current binding) plus some generalization of operator overloading support for the arrow ("->") and dot (".") operators in the definition of C++, or (2) an ODBMS implementation architecture that allows the normal dereference code generated by the C++ compiler to work for persistent as well as transient objects. Some vendors may support systems in which object creation, deletion, and reference; attribute value get and set; relationship traversal; and operation invocation use the standard C++ syntax for working on transient objects, but their query language embedding will be a call to the oql function, passing the query as a string.

There are two paths for moving applications written to the current binding to the future binding: (1) make no change, since implementations supporting the future binding continue to support the current binding also or (2) use tools to automatically translate source code to subsequent bindings.

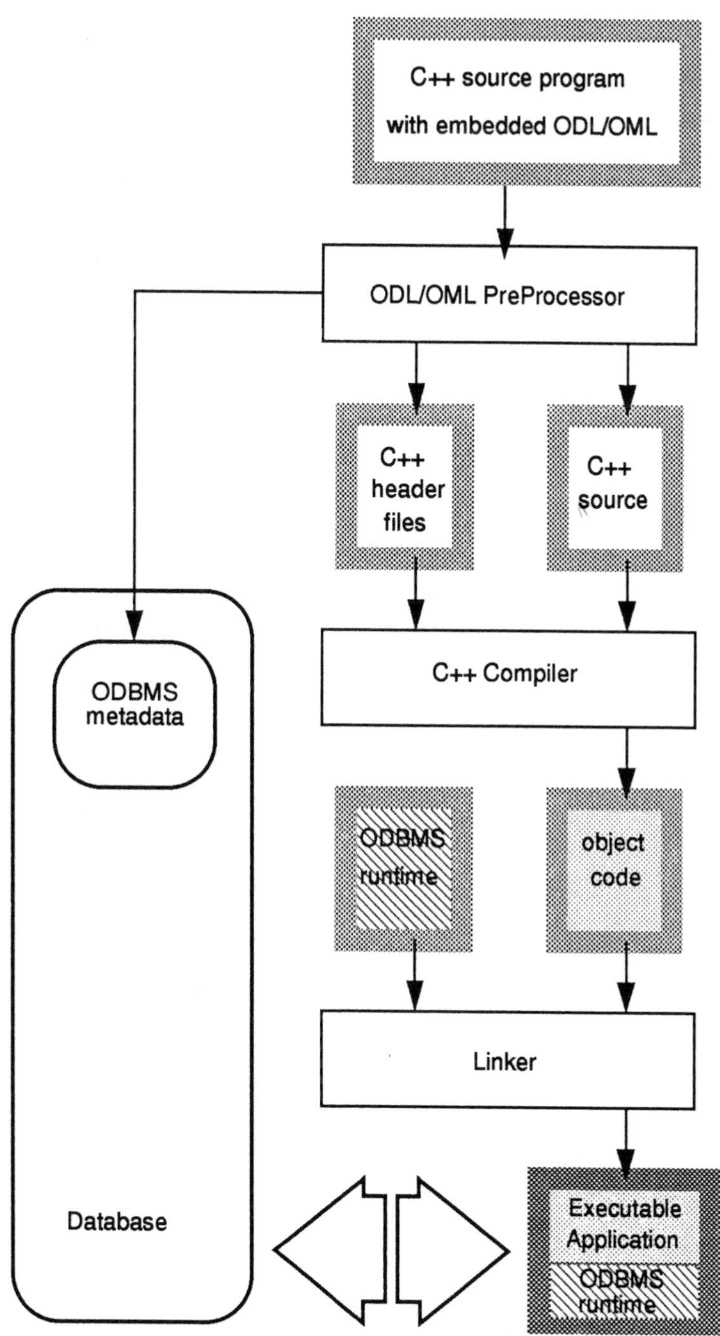

Figure 5-4. Future Preprocessor Steps

Chapter 6

Smalltalk Binding

6.1 Introduction

This chapter defines the Smalltalk binding for the ODMG Object Model, ODL and OQL. As with our C++ work, our objective here is to bind to Smalltalk in a natural way, consistent with the principles of the Smalltalk language. The ODMG Smalltalk binding is based on the principle that Smalltalk programmers should feel they are using one language, not two separate languages with arbitrary boundaries between them. The principle has several implications that are evident in the design of the Smalltalk binding described in the body of this chapter:

1. There is a unified type system shared by Smalltalk and the ODBMS; individual instances of common types can be persistent or transient.
2. The binding respects the Smalltalk syntax.
3. The binding respects the fact that Smalltalk is untyped and inherently dynamic, and does not force the strong typing of the Object Model (see Chapter 2) into the Smalltalk environment. The opportunity for strong type checking is left to the ODBMS.

The ODMG binding for Smalltalk is still evolving. We decided, however, that it was worth including to show the flavor of use of ODBMSs with Smalltalk, to emphasize the multi-lingual nature of our Object Model, ODL and OQL work, and to establish a foundation for further work. Any and all comments on the Smalltalk binding are especially welcomed.

Smalltalk Images[1] provide a form of object persistence, but are not the same as databases. For example, Smalltalk Images do not implement important database features such as sharing of objects among multiple users and applications or support of transactions, crash recovery, and so forth.

Smalltalk implements its own memory management and expects all Smalltalk objects to exist within its object space. A Smalltalk object cannot refer to memory outside this

---

1. A running Smalltalk system is composed of two parts: an executable Virtual Machine (VM) and an Image. The VM is an execution engine that controls method binding and execution of compiled code. The Image is an integrated in-memory object repository. In Smalltalk everything is an object, including low--level data types such as integers and compiled Smalltalk code. The Image is a bound set of objects that are tightly interrelated. The user can at any time save a new or modified Image and may start Smalltalk with any previously saved Image. This feature provides a sort of poor man's all-in-one persistence that is inherent in the language itself.

space via a direct pointer. Thus Smalltalk cannot directly reference objects within an ODBMS cache. This means that in all likelihood an ODMG Smalltalk binding will be implemented through external (C) procedures.

The ODMG Smalltalk binding is based on the Smalltalk Object and Class instance protocols, along with new classes DatabaseGlobals and Session. The ODMG Smalltalk binding adds:

- constraint: argument arrays containing type definitions for class properties
- to the Class instance protocol: methods for adding and removing keys
- to the Object instance protocol: methods relating to creating and modifying persistent objects
- a subclass of the Smalltalk global dictionary class for object names
- a Session class, which contains methods for connecting to databases and controlling transactions

6.2 Smalltalk ODL

This section describes the binding of ODMG ODL to Smalltalk. Smalltalk ODL provides a description of the database schema as a set of object classes, including their attributes, relationships, and operations. The Smalltalk binding for ODL has a syntactic style that is consistent with the declarative aspects of the Smalltalk language. Instances of these classes can be manipulated using Smalltalk and the Smalltalk OML (see Section 6.3). Smalltalk is an inherently dynamic language with dynamic typing and runtime class definition. Thus the Smalltalk ODL is dynamic and is closely related to Smalltalk OML. For the most part it makes sense to refer to them together as a single language, Smalltalk ODL/OML.

The example below shows a sample object type declaration including property type declarations and operation type declarations. As Smalltalk is a dynamic language, operations need not be specified at object type declaration time. For this reason, operation declarations are not present in the folowing object type declaration as seen by the Smalltalk Browser:

```
Object subclass: 'Professor'
instVarNames: #('age', 'name', 'salary','universityId', 'dept' , 'advisees')
classVars: #()
poolDictionaries: #()
inDictionary: ADictionary
constraints: #(#('age', SmallInteger),
   #('name', String),
   #('salary', Money),
   #('universityId',Integer),
   #('dept',Department, 'inverse', 'professors'),
     #('advisees',StudentSet, 'inverse', 'advisor', 'orderedBy','studentId'))
```

We use the Smalltalk class definition facilities directly. The constraints: argument array contains type definitions for implementations of both attributes and relationships. The class compiler detects these constraint types and generates appropriate methods to support the attribute and relationship semantics. When the constraints: argument array contains a single class name, e.g., constraints: #(SmallInteger), then the constraint is on the varying array or collection part of instances of the class.

The only types that can be embedded as objects within a class are Char and SmallInteger. All other types are treated by Smalltalk as first-class objects. Let's now consider the declaration of class characteristics: attributes, relationships, and operations.

6.2.1 Class Properties

Class properties are those that characterize the class itself, rather than any of its individual instances. There are three class properties specifiable in Smalltalk ODL: (1) the supertype of a class, (2) the extent of a class, and (3) the properties ("keys") whose values uniquely distinguish one instance of a class from another.

Any Smalltalk class is persistence-capable. There is no need to distinguish syntactically between classes that may or may not instantiate themselves with persistent instances.

6.2.1.1 Subtypes

The subtype hierarchy is described using the usual Smalltalk subclass creation messages:

```
superClassName subclass: #subClassName
```

For example

```
Object subclass: #Person
Person subclass: #Professor
Person subclass: #Student
```

Smalltalk supports only single inheritance, not multiple inheritance. Thus Smalltalk cannot implement the full ODMG Object Model, as it includes multiple inheritance. If there is a need to share C++ objects with the Smalltalk environment, then multiple inheritance should be avoided in the C++ environment. This specification does not address the resolution of these complications.

The ODMG Object Model and ODL support the optional specification of the extent of a class, which is the set of all of its instances. Smalltalk inherently supports the notion of extents through the allInstances method, which is defined on the class class and answers an ordered collection of all the instances of the class. For example:

```
allSailboats := Sailboat allInstances.
```

The allInstances method is executed on the Sailboat object, which is the instance of the class class containing information about the Sailboat class. The result is returned as an ordered collection named allSailboats; this is the extent. The binding does not introduce explicit extent protocols. The Smalltalk iterators defined on ordered collections can be used to run through all the elements of the ordered collection answered by the allInstances method.

Note that the extent created using allInstances contains both transient and persistent instances. Extents that contain only persistent instances are not part of the Smalltalk binding of ODMG-93. If there is a requirement for extents to include just persistent instances, then either the allInstances method could be overloaded for persistent objects, or the ODBMS could separately maintain persistent extents and would probably implement them as weak arrays. An object would be placed in such an extent either when it receives the persist message or when it is attached to a persistent object. If supported by the ODBMS, persistent extents should be implemented in such a way that insert and remove operations are not available for use by application developers.

A persistent-instances only extent could be specified at class creation time using a method defined on the class class and implemented by the ODBMS:

```
persistentExtent: 'extentname'
persistentExtentTrue
  persistentExtentFalse
```

The persistentExtent method answers an ordered collection.

6.2.1.2 Keys

A Smalltalk program can request that the values of a property uniquely identify persistent instances of a class by specifying that the property be a key. A class may have zero or more keys. An ODBMS may elect to construct an index on each key. A key must be a literal-valued attribute or list of literal-valued attributes.

A key is requested by sending an addkey message to the class's class object, with the keyed property as the argument. addkey is provided as part of the ODBMS API as a method defined on the class class. In contrast to the C++ ODL/OML, keys are requested dynamically using the Smalltalk ODL/OML. The syntax is:

```
className addKey: #symbol
```

or

```
className addKey: #(symbol1, symbol2, ...)
```

For example:

```
Sailboat addKey: #registrationId.
Sailboat addKey: #slipNo.
Section addKey: #(courseNo, sectionNo).
```

The uniqueness of a key's value is enforced by the ODBMS over the collection of persistent instances of the class.

To find an object with a particular key value, the Smalltalk select method is used directly. For example

```
thisSailboat := Sailboat allInstances select: [:aBoat | aBoat slipNo = 1234].
```

This statement will answer the instance of Sailboat whose slipNo value is 1234. For a persistent class, the select method would be overridden and forwarded to the ODBMS or translated into a query. The ODBMS may use an index, if appropriate, in filtering the instances.

A uniqueness constraint can be removed using the removeKey method, which is again defined by the ODBMS on the class class. For example:

```
Sailboat removeKey: #registrationId.
```

6.2.2 Instance Properties

6.2.2.1 Attributes

The untyped, dynamic nature of Smalltalk makes the language inherently different in philosophy from (1) the ODMG Object Model, which focuses on explicit semantics, (2) ODBMSs, which generally implement strong typing, and (3) C++, which is weakly typed and static. The Smalltalk ODL binding uses the Smalltalk constraint syntax to add typing to persistent objects in a manner that is consistent with the Smalltalk paradigm.

We expect that the typical Smalltalk database development environment will use graphical tools to define database schemas. These environments do not even need an ODL binding to Smalltalk; they might instead use an ASCII-based form of ODL for schema interchange.

Smalltalk ODL expects attribute type declarations to be passed to the ODBMS using the constraint: arguments array capability of Smalltalk. Each attribute declaration is a Symbol, Type pair, which the ODBMS uses to enforce typing on persistent objects. The syntax is:

```
constraints: #(...
    #(attributeName1, type1),
    #(attributeName2, type2), ...)
```

For example,

```
constraints: #(#('name', String),
    #('salary', Money),
    #('facultyId', Integer), ...
```

When the ODBMS encounters a two-parametered constraint of this form, it knows that the second parameter specifies the type to be enforced on the instance variable named in the first parameter. In the example above, the value of the name attribute must be of type String. The value of the salary attribute must be of type Money. The value of the facultyId attribute must be of type Integer. If a constraint is violated, the ODBMS should raise an exception.

6.2.2.2 Relationships

Relationships between objects are defined in Smalltalk ODL using the same constraint mechanism used for attribute declarations. The general syntax for a relationship traversal path declaration is:

```
constraints: #(
    #(traversalPathName1, targetType
        ,'inverse', traversalPathName2
            [, 'orderBy', attributeList] ))
```

For example,

```
Object subclass: #Professor
instVarNames: #('dept', 'advisees')
constraints: #(#('dept', Department,'inverse', 'professors'),
    #('advisees',StudentSet,'inverse','advisor','orderBy','studentId'))
```

The basic new operator is overloaded by the ODBMS to use these self constraints. The constraints are interpreted to initialize the newly created object correctly.

- If the constraint entry has two parameters (i.e., for an attribute declaration), the ODBMS uses the type information to verify that only the correct kinds of values are assigned to the attribute. If the second parameter is a collection, then the ODBMS interprets the traversal path as 1-to-many and initializes it to a set of nil pointers rather than a single nil pointer.
- If the constraint entry has four parameters (i.e., for a traversal path with an inverse, but no ordering specification), the ODBMS uses the type information to ensure that only references to the correct kinds of instances are placed in instances of the traversal path. Additionally the name of the inverse traversal path is stored as part of the ODBMS metadata.
- If the constraint entry has six parameters (i.e., for a traversal path with target instances sequenced by the values of one or more of their attributes), the ODBMS uses the type information as above and the ordering information is stored as part of the ODBMS metadata. These metadata are used when a programmer attempts to add a target member to a traversal path instance.

From the database and Object Model points of view, it would be desirable for the ODBMS to enforce the semantics of relationships within a running Smalltalk Image, whether the reference is between persistent objects or involves transient instances.

However, strong type enforcement is inconsistent with the classical Smalltalk paradigm, and therefore is enforced only by the ODBMS and for relationships between persistent instances. Constraints are executed by the ODBMS, not by Smalltalk.

6.2.3 Operations

Operation declarations are defined using the usual Smalltalk syntax.

6.2.4 Example Smalltalk ODL Binding

The ODL example from Section 3.3 can be bound to Smalltalk as follows:

```
Object subclass: #Course
instVarNames: #('name','number','hasSections',
        'hasPrerequisites','isPrerequisiteFor')
constraints:#(
    #('name',String),
    #('number',String),
    #('hasSections',SectionSet,'inverse','course','orderBy','number'),
    #('hasPrerequisites',CourseSet,'inverse','isPrerequisiteFor'),
    #('isPrerequisiteFor',CourseSet,'inverse','hasPrerequisite'))

Object subclass: #Section
instVarNames: #('number','isTaughtBy','hasTA','isSectionOf',
        'isTakenBy')
constraints:#(
    #('number',String),
    #('isTaughtBy',Professor,'inverse','teaches'),
    #('hasTA',TA,'inverse','assists'),
    #('isSectionOf',Course,'inverse','sections'),
    #('isTakenBy',StudentSet,'inverse','takes'))

Object subclass: #Employee
instVarNames: #('name','id','annualSalary'')
constraints:#(
    #('name',String),
    #('id',Integer),
    #('annualSalary',Integer))

Employee subclass: #Professor
instVarNames: #('rank','teaches')
constraints:#(
    #('rank',#(Enum,#('full','associate','assistant'))),
```

```
    #('teaches',SectionSet,'inverse','isTaughtBy'))

Student subclass: #TA
instVarNames: #('assists')
constraints:#(
    #('assists',Section,'inverse','hasTA'))

Object subclass:#Student
instVarNames:#('name','studentId','dormAddress','takes')
constraints:#
    #('name',String),
    #('studentId',String),
    #('dormAddress',#(Struct,
            #('college',String,'roomNumber',String))),
    #('takes',SectionSet,' inverse',' isTakenBy'))
```

Note that the example has been simplified a bit to avoid the multiple inheritance present in the ODL specification of Chapter 3.

6.3 Smalltalk OML

This section defines the Smalltalk Object Manipulation Language (OML). The overriding guiding principle in the design of Smalltalk OML is that the syntax used to create, delete, identify, reference, get/set property values, and invoke operations on a persistent object should be no different from that used for objects of shorter lifetimes. A single expression may freely intermix references to persistent and transient objects. Smalltalk OML will typically be implemented as a class library, as a preprocessor approach is incompatible with the dynamic nature of Smalltalk. All Smalltalk OML operations are invoked by sending messages to appropriate methods.

6.3.1 Object creation and deletion

6.3.1.1 Object creation

Both transient and persistent objects are created in the usual way by sending the message new to the appropriate class. Persistence is not limited to any particular subset of the class hierarchy, nor is it determined at object creation time. To make an object persistent, send the message **persist** to the object; **persist** creates in the database a persistent object corresponding to the Smalltalk receiver object and answers **self**. At the next commit, that object will be stored in a database. For example:

```
mySailboat := Sailboat new.
  mySailboat persist.
```

The ODBMS overloads the new method to correctly initialize the instance, checking its constraint array parameters and setting parameters to nil appropriately.

A transient object that participates in a relationship with a persistent object also becomes persistent when a transaction commit occurs. This approach is sometimes called transitive persistence.

6.3.1.2 Object Deletion

In Smalltalk there is no notion of explicit deletion of objects. Rather an object is removed from the Image during Smalltalk garbage collection if that object is not referenced by any other object. In keeping with the Smalltalk philosophy, ODMG-93 does not add a notion of explicit deletion in the Smalltalk binding.

6.3.2 Naming

The ODBMS implements a global dictionary, called DatabaseGlobals, as a subclass of the Smalltalk global dictionary class. DatabaseGlobals contains the names of all named persistent objects. To name an object add an association to the dictionary using the usual Smalltalk add message or an at/put pair on the Dictionary class. The general syntax is:

```
DatabaseGlobals add: (Association key: #myNewName value: anObjectId)
```

or equivalently

```
DatabaseGlobals at: #myNewName put: anObjectId
```

Similarly, a name can be removed from the dictionary using the removeAssociation message:

```
DatabaseGlobals removeAssociation: (Association key: #myOldName
  value:anObjectId)
```

or equivalently

```
DatabaseGlobals removeKey: #myOldName
```

To locate an object with a particular key value use the usual Smalltalk access to a dictionary, answering the object of desire:

```
anObject := DatabaseGlobals at:#myName ifAbsent: [ ...]
```

6.3.3 Object Modification

A persistent object is automatically swapped into the Smalltalk Image whenever it is sent a message. A persistent object in the Image can be modified using the normal Smalltalk mechanisms. It is desirable that there be no distinction between modifications of transient and persistent objects. However, until all Smalltalk implementations support the necessary infrastructure, it may be necessary to treat transient and persistent objects slightly differently.

Modified persistent Smalltalk objects will have their updated values automatically reflected in the ODBMS at transaction commit. This also applies to modified persistent objects that are garbage collected from within a running Smalltalk Image.

In as much as not all of the commercial Smalltalk implementations support the necessary functionality to provide transparent updating of persistent objects (weak arrays, notification, and compiler access), a markModified interface may be provided for these Smalltalks. Within such interfaces, persistent objects to be modified are sent the message markModified; markModified prepares the receiver object for modification by setting a write lock (if it does not already have a write lock) and marking it so that the ODBMS can detect that the object has been modified. Marking an object using markModified means that the object will be posted to the database at the next commit.

In systems that require this special treatment of persistent objects, it is conventional to send the markModified message as part of the method that sets the attribute value. The ODBMS will call markModified implicitly as part of the persist operation (which makes an instance persistent).

An immutable object (value), such as an instance of Character and SmallInteger and instances such as nil, true, and false, cannot change its intrinsic value. The markModified message is ignored by these objects. Sending markModified to a transient object is also a null operation.

6.3.4 Transactions

Transactions are implemented in Smalltalk within the scope of a session, which is a period of active connection to a database. Transactions are dynamically scoped. Transactions can be started, committed, aborted, and checkpointed. Transactions must be explicitly started. They may be nested, but all transactions in the nest must be handled using a single concurrency control policy. The default standard policy is pessimistic concurrency control, but an ODBMS may support additional policies as well. With the pessimistic policy all access, creation, modification, and deletion of persistent objects must be done within a transaction.

A transaction is started by invoking the beginTransaction method on an instance of the Session class:

```
aSession beginTransaction.
```

Transient objects are not subject to transaction semantics. Committing a transaction does not remove transient objects from memory. Aborting a transaction does not restore the state of modified transient objects.

A transaction is committed by sending a commitTransaction message to the Session object. Committing a transaction writes the changes to persistent objects to a database and ends the current transaction. An exception is raised if the commit is unsuccessful. For example:

```
aSession commitTransaction.
```

A transaction may also be checkpointed, which means that all modified persistent objects are committed to the database, locks are retained, and persistent objects are retained in memory:

```
aSession checkpointTransaction.
```

This can be useful in order to continue working with the same objects, while ensuring that intermediate logical results are written to the database. The ODBMS is responsible for synchronizing the cache with the database.

A transaction is aborted by sending an abortTransaction message to a Session object. For example:

```
aSession abortTransaction.
```

The transaction is ended, changes made to persistent objects since the last commit are abandoned, and locks are released.

Transactions may be nested. The commit of inner transactions is only relative to the outermost transaction. That is, the changes made in the inner transactions only commit if all the containing outer transactions also commit. If an inner transaction commits and the outer transaction aborts, the changes made in the inner transaction are aborted as well.

Unless explicitly specified, objects activated into memory are locked with the default lock for the active concurrency control policy. In this standard the default lock for both pessimistic and optimistic concurrency control is a readLock. A lock can optionally be explicitly acquired on an object by sending a message to that object, with the mode of the lock as the argument.

```
anObject acquireLock: #aLockModeSymbol
locks := LockSet at: self ifAbsent:[LockSet at:self put:Set new]
locks add:#aLockModeSymbol
```

For example:

```
mySailboat acquireLock: #write.
```

The specified kind of lock is acquired on the receiver. An exception is raised if the requested lock cannot be granted.

To test whether a write lock can be granted on an object and then to set the lock:

```
anObject writable ((LockSet at:self) ifAbsent: [#(...)]) includes:#write) not
```

Locks are released implicitly at the end of the transaction, unless the option to retain locks is used.

6.3.5 Database Operations

6.3.5.1 Database Open

To open a database, send an openDatabase message to a Session instance, with the name of the database as its argument.

```
aSession openDatabase: #databaseName.
```

For example

```
aSession openDatabase: #myDatabase.
```

This method locates the named database and makes the appropriate connection. An exception is raised if the open is not successful. A Smalltalk program must open a database before accessing any persistent objects in that database. An ODBMS implementor may choose to provide optional keywords on the openDatabase for user authorization and validation.

6.3.5.2 Database Close

To close a database, send a closeDatabase message to the Session instance, parameterized by the name of the database to be closed:

```
aSession closeDatabase: #databaseName.
```

This method drops the connection to the open database. A Smalltalk exception is raised if the close is unsuccessful. After a database is closed, further attempts to access objects in the database will raise an exception. If the databaseName parameter is omitted, the most recently opened database connection is dropped.

6.4 Smalltalk OQL

Smalltalk OQL implements the OQL operations on collections as defined in Chapter 4, using the Smalltalk methods defined on collections. For example:

```
Sailboat allInstances select: [:sb | sb noMasts = 2]
```

answers first an ordered collection of all instances of the Sailboat class, then applies the select method, which executes the block that filters qualifying instances, i.e., those for sailboats with two masts. A slightly more complex query is:

```
Sailboat allInstances select: [:sb | sb noMasts = 2 &
                                    (sb sails includes: #jib)]
```

This filters the qualifying instances of the Sailboat extent to those with two masts and a jib sail. Two queries in sequence are:

```
racingSailboats := Sailboat allInstances select: [:sb | sb sails size > 10]
cruisingSailboats := Sailboat allInstances reject: [:sb | racingSailboats
                                                    includes: sb]
```

6.5 Future Binding

We expect the ODMG Smalltalk binding to evolve to provide a strongly typed Smalltalk with object persistence. Various approaches are under consideration for making type checking a shared responsibility of Smalltalk and the ODBMS. For example, we could introduce a variant on the subclass creation message with an additional keyword -- instPropertyTypes -- which is positionally last. This keyword would be used to define the attributes and relationships of the type. For example,

```
Object subclass: #Professor
instPropertyTypes: '
   age <SmallInteger>
   name <String>
   salary <Money>
   universityId <SmallInteger>
   dept <Department> inverse <professors>
     advisees <List <Student>> inverse <advisor> orderBy <studentId>'
Object subclass: #Student
instPropertyTypes: '
   studentId <SmallInteger>
   lastName <String>
   advisor <Professor> inverse <advisees>
     classes <Set <Course>> inverse <studentsEnrolled>'
Object subclass: #Course
instPropertyTypes: '
   courseNo <SmallInteger>
   courseName <String>
   studentsEnrolled <List <Student>> inverse <classes>
         orderBy <lastName>'
```

Other considerations for the future binding include treating attributes and relationships as first class types. A step toward accomplishing this might be to establish a Pool dictionary of relationships which are themselves dictionaries. Ordering could be accomplished by defining the dictionary class to produce the desired sequencing on fetches. The keys then become dictionary entries, with the element of the varying part holding the related values themselves.

The future binding may include more precise treatment of scoping. For example, in addition to the DatabaseGlobals class introduced in this Smalltalk binding, the future binding may introduce a UserGlobals class, for instances which are persistent but within the domain of a particular user. If the Object Model evolves to handling multiple name scopes, then that capability will also be added to the Smalltalk binding.

The future binding will probably be more precise about the treatment of transient instances in extents and enforcement of key constraints (i.e., uniqueness constraints). The current binding includes both transient and persistent instances in an extent because extents are supported through the Smalltalk allInstances method. The future binding may introduce an overloaded version of the allInstances method, to include just persistent instances. The current binding enforces uniqueness constraints only over persistent instances, while the future binding may also include keys that cover transient instances as well.

The ODMG C++ binding includes notions of deleting objects. Explicit deletion has been omitted from the Smalltalk binding because of unresolved questions about marrying explicit deletion with the Smalltalk notions of garbage collection. For example, what should happen to transitive closures in which an explicitly deleted object participates? If the deleted object is a root object and objects in its transitive closure are not referenced by any other objects, should these objects also be deleted, since they cannot be reached? Can an application correctly predict the impact of deleting an object, especially if the relationships form an acyclic directed graph or if recursive relationships are involved? Some of these issues may be addressed to incorporate a form of explicit deletion in a future ODMG Smalltalk binding.

The current Smalltalk binding is incomplete in its mapping of Object Model Structured_Object types to the built-in classes of Smalltalk. This correspondence may be included in future binding work.

The current Smalltalk binding is also incomplete in its treatment of OQL and query specification. This is an area of candidate work for the future binding.

Appendix A

Comparison with OMG Object Model

A.1 Introduction

This appendix compares the ODMG Object Model outlined in Chapter 2 of this specification with the OMG Object Model as outlined in Chapter 4 of the *OMG Architecture Guide*.

The bottom line is that the ODMG Object Model (ODMG/OM) is a superset of the OMG Object Model (OMG/OM).

The subsections of this appendix discuss the purpose of the two models, how the ODMG/OM fits into the component/profile structure defined by the OMG/OM, and review the capability between the two models in the major areas defined by the OMG/OM: types, instances, objects, and operations.

A.2 Purpose

The OMG/OM states that its primary objective is to support application portability. Three levels of portability are called out: (1) design portability, (2) source code portability, and (3) object code portability. The OMG/OM focused on design portability. The ODMG/OM goes a step further — to source code portability. The OMG/OM distinguishes two other dimensions of portability: portability across technology domains (e.g., a common object model across GUI, PL, and DBMS domains), and portability across products from different vendors within a technology domain (e.g., across ODBMS products from different vendors). The ODMG/OM focuses on portability within the technology domain of object database management systems. The ODMG standards suite is designed to allow application builders to write to a single ODBMS application programming interface (API), in the assurance that this API will be supported by a wide range of ODBMS vendors. The ODMG/OM defines the semantics of the object types that make up this API. Subsequent chapters within the ODMG standard define the syntactic forms through which this model is bound to specific programming languages.

To offer real portabililty, a standard has to support a level of DBMS functionality rich enough to meet the needs of the applications expected to use the standard. It cannot define such a low-level API that real applications need to use functionality supplied only by vendor-specific extensions to the API. The low-level, least-common-denominator approach taken in the standards for relational data management has meant that real applications need to use functionality supplied only by vendor-specific extensions to the API. Several studies in the late 1980s that analyzed large bodies of applications written against the relational API (SQL) showed that 30-40% of the RDBMS calls in the application are actually "standard SQL"; the other 60- 70% use vendor-specific extensions. The result is that the relational standard does not in practice deliver the source-code-level application portability that it promised. The ODMG APIs have been designed to provide a much higher level of functionality and therefore a much higher degree of application portability.

A.3 Components and Profiles

The OMG Object Model is broken into a set of *components*, with a distinguished "Core Component" that defines objects and operations. The theory espoused by the OMG is that each "technology domain" (GUI, ODBMS, etc.) will assemble a set of these components into a *profile*. Figure A-1 illustrates this. Two profiles are shown —the Object Request Broker (ORB) profile and the Object DBMS (ODBMS) profile.

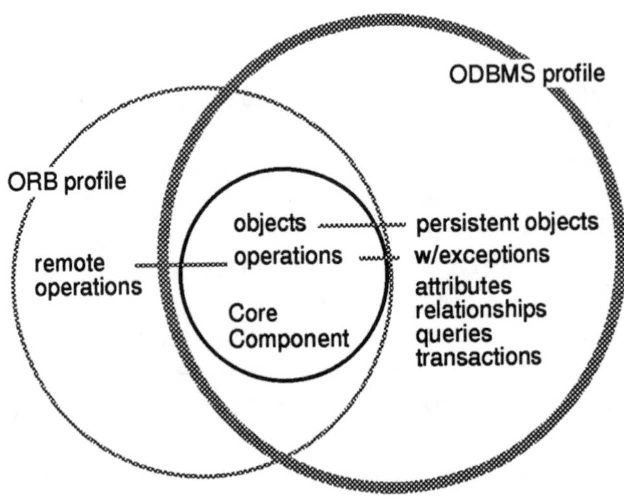

Figure A-1

The ORB profile includes the Core Component plus support for remote operations. The ODBMS profile includes the Core Component plus support for:

- persistent objects
- properties (attributes and relationships)
- queries
- transactions

It also strengthens the core component definition of operations by including exception returns.

To date, the only OMG/OM component that has been defined is the Core Component. The additional functionality included in the ORB profile has not been formally specified as a set of named components. Nor are there OMG component definitions for the functionality expected to be added by the ODBMS profile. One of the reasons for making the comparison between the OMG/OM (i.e., the Core Component) is that the members of ODMG expect to submit definitions of each of the items in the bulleted list above as candidate *components*, and the sum of them as a candidate *profile* for object database management systems. Since the submitting companies collectively represent 80+% of the commercially available ODBMS products on the market, we assume that adoption of an ODBMS profile along the lines of that outlined in Chapter 2 will move through the OMG process relatively quickly.

The OMG/OM is outlined in bullet form below, with indications how the ODMG/OM agrees.

Types, Instances, Interfaces, and Implementations:

- Objects are instances of types.
- A type defines the behavior and state of its instances.
- Behavior is specified as a set of operations.
- An object can be an immediate instance of only one type.
- The type of an object is determined statically at the time the object is created; objects do not dynamically acquire and lose types.
- Types are organized into a subtype/supertype graph.
- A type may have multiple supertypes.
- Supertypes are explicitly specified; subtype/supertype relationships between types are not deduced from signature compatibility of the types.

Operations:

- Operations have signatures that specify the operation name, arguments, and return values.
- Operations are defined on a single type — the type of their distinguished first argument — rather than on two types.
- Operations may take either literals or objects as their arguments. Semantics of argument passing is pass by reference.

- Operations are invoked.
- Operations may have side effects.
- Operations are implemented by methods in the implementation portion of the type definition.

The OMG/OM does not currently define exception returns on operations; it says that it expects there to be an exception-handling component defined outside of the core model. The ODMG/OM does define exception returns to operations.

A.4 Type Hierarchy

The fact that the ODMG/OM is a superset of the OMG/OM can also be seen by looking at the built-in type hierarchy defined by the two models. Figure A-2 shows the ODMG/OM type hierarchy. The types whose names are shown in italics are those which are also defined in the OMG/OM. As in Chapter 2, indenting is used to show subtype/supertype relationships, e.g., the type Structured_Object is a subtype of the type Object.

- Denotable_Object
  - *Object*
    - Atomic_Object
    - Structured_Object
  - *Literal (Non-Object in OMG/OM)*
    - Atomic_Literal
    - Structured_Literal
- Characteristic
  - Property
    - Attribute
    - Relationship
  - *Operation*

Figure A-2

The ODMG/OM is a richer model than the OMG/OM — particularly in its support for properties and in its more detailed development of a subtype hierarchy below the types Object and Literal. The only differences between the two models in the areas common to them are two type names. The type that is called Literal in the ODMG/OM is called Non-Object in the OMG/OM. Although the OMG/OM does not formally introduce a supertype of the types Object and Non-Object, in the body of the document it refers to instances of these two types as the set of all "denotable values" or "Dvals" in the model.

In the ODMG/OM a common supertype for Object and Literal is defined. It is called Denotable_Object. Its instances are the set of all denotable objects. The instances of type Object are mutable; they are therefore given OIDs in the ODMG/OM; although the value of the object may change, its OID is invariant. The OID can therefore be used to denote the object. Literals, by contrast, are immutable. Since the instances of a literal type are distinguished from one another by their value, this value can be used directly to denote the instance. There is no need to ascribe to literals separate OIDS.

In summary, the ODMG/OM is a clean superset of the OMG/OM.

A.5 The ORB profile

A second question could be raised. One product category has already been approved by the OMG — the ORB. To what extent are the noncore components implicit in that product consistent or inconsistent with their counterpart noncore components in the ODMG/OM? There is some divergence in literals, inheritance semantics, and operations — the latter because the ORB restricts in two key ways the semantics already defined in the OMG core object model: object identity and the semantics of arguments passed to operations. Those battles, however, are not ours. They are between the OMG ORB task force and the OMG Object Model task force. The requirement placed on a prospective ODBMS task force is simply that the set of components included in the ODBMS profile include the Core Component — objects and operations. This appendix addresses that question.

A.6 Other Standards Groups

There are several standards organizations that are in the process of defining object models. These include:

1. Application-specific standards groups that have defined an object model as a basis for their work in defining schemas of common types in their application domain, e.g.,
   - CFI (electrical CAD)
   - PDES/STEP (mechanical CAD)
   - ODA (computer-aided publishing)
   - PCTE (CASE)
   - OSI/NMF (telephony)
   - ANSI X3H6 (CASE)
   - ANSI X3H4 (IRDS reference model)

2. Formal standards bodies working on generic object models, e.g.,
    - ISO ODP
    - ANSI X3H7 (Object Information Systems)
    - ANSI X3T5.4 (managed objects)
    - ANSI X3T3

It is our current working assumption that the OMG-promulgated interface definitions for ORB and ODBMS will have sufficiently broad support across software vendors and hardware manufacturers that interface definitions put in the public domain through the OMG and supported by commercial vendors will develop the kind of de facto market share that has historically been an important prerequisite to adoption by ANSI and ISO. Should that prove not to be the case, the ODMG will make direct proposals to ANSI and ISO once the member companies of ODMG and their customers have developed a base of experience with the proposed API through use of commercial ODBMS products that support this API.

Appendix B

ODBMS in the OMG ORB Environment

B.1 Introduction

The existing documents of OMG do not yet address the issue of how an ODBMS fits into the OMG environment and, in particular, how it communicates with and cooperates with the ORB. This fundamental architectural issue is critical to the success of users of the OMG environment who also need ODBMSs.

This document is a position statement of the ODMG defining the desired architecture. It explicitly does not discuss the architecture of the internals of an ODBMS implementation but rather leaves that to the implementor of the ODBMS. Instead, it discusses how the ODBMS fits architecturally into the larger OMG environment.

The issues for a successful fit are the following.

- performance — e.g., direct object access
- distribution and heterogeneity — as managed by ODBMS for fine-grained objects
- ODBMS as Object Manager — responsible for multiple objects.
- common repository — ability of ORB to use ODBMS as repository
- ODBMS as a user of the ORB — ability of ODBMS to use the services provided by the ORB (including other ODBMSs).

The architecture must support ODBMS implementations and client interfaces to achieve these.

B.2 Roles for the ORB and ODBMS

The ORB and the ODBMS are different. The ODBMS's role in the OMG environment is to support definition, creation, and manipulation with the services of persistence, transactions, recovery, and concurrent sharing for application objects varying from the smallest units (e.g., words in a word processor, cells or formula terms in a spreadsheet) to the largest (e.g., documents, systems). Many applications desire these services to include, within a single vendor product, transparent distribution in a heterogeneous mixture of platforms and other services such as versioning and security.

Note that we define ODBMS according to the services it provides, not according to any particular implementation of those services. Radically different implementations are possible, including not only traditional ODBMS approaches, but also file-based approaches, each offering different levels of services and trade-offs.

The ORB provides a larger-scale set of services across heterogeneous vendors and products; e.g., it allows clients to use multiple ODBMSs. The service it provides is behavior invocation, or method dispatch. In contrast, the ODBMS provides a single-vendor capability and only a specific set of services rather than arbitrary ones; however, those services include more detailed capabilities of high-performance, fine-grained persistence that are used directly within applications to support millions of primitive objects. The ORB, when it needs persistence services, could choose to implement them via use of an ODBMS. The ODBMS services may be invoked via the ORB.

B.3 Issues

Here we describe some of the key issues that this architecture must address. Since the ODBMS supports millions of fine-grained objects used directly by the applications, it must provide high-performance access to those objects. The pertinent characteristic differentiating large- and small-grain objects is access time. If an application is accessing only one or two objects (e.g., open a spreadsheet document), there is little concern for the time to communicate across networks through the ORB. However, if the application is accessing thousands or millions of objects (e.g., formulae and variables in cells in the spreadsheet), system overhead becomes a significant factor as perceived by the user.

In many cases this means access time that is comparable to native in-memory object usage. To provide this, the ODBMS must be able to move objects as necessary in the distributed environment and cache them locally in the address space of the application, if desired, and in efficient format.

Since the ODBMS objects are those used primarily within the application, it is desirable to support an interface that is natural and direct to the user.

Examples of applications and object granularities for which ODBMS services must be available and efficient include: spreadsheets; word processors; documents of these; primitive elements within these such as cells, formulae, variables, words, phrases, and formatting specifications; network managers with objects representing machines, users, and sessions; resource allocation schemes; CAD and CAM with objects such as circuits and gates and pins, routing traces, form features, bezier curves, finite element mesh nodes, edges and faces, tool paths, simulation, and analysis support; financial portfolio analysis; and so on. There may be millions of such objects, in complex interconnected networks of relationships.

The interfaces to those objects must be defined in such a way as to allow ORB access when appropriate (e.g., for cross-database-vendor object relationships) or direct use of the ODBMS (e.g., for objects with no need to publish themselves for public use through the ORB). This should be done with a single interface to allow transparency to the client and to allow the client to choose to vary functionality as desired.

The ODBMS acts as manager of many objects, so the architecture and interfaces must allow such assignment of responsibilities. The ODBMS can provide distribution of objects among multiple and potentially heterogeneous platforms, so the architecture and implementation must allow this functionality to be relegated to the ODBMS.

The ORB and other OMG components (service providers, library facilities, service users, etc.) may need the services of persistence, or management of objects that exist beyond process lifetimes, for various kinds of objects, including type-defining objects and instances of these. It is desirable, architecturally, to consolidate common services in a common shared component. The architecture must allow use of an ODBMS for this purpose in order to take advantage both of the capabilities it provides and integration with other OMG components using the same services.

As mentioned above, different ODBMS implementation approaches must be supported. The architecture and the OMG interfaces must provide a single interface (or set of interfaces) that allows use of a wide variety of such implementations. A single interface allows users to choose which implementation to use and when. This should cover not only full ODBMS implementations but other approaches with partial functionality, such as file management approaches.

In addition to direct use of an ODBMS through an interface such as that defined in the ODMG-93 specification, an ODBMS could be decomposed in order to implement a number of semi-independent *services*, such as persistence, transactions, relationships, and versions. The OMG Object Services Task Force is defining such services. This is an area for future work by the object database vendors.

In addition to the ORB and users of the ORB accessing ODBMSs, it is also the case that an ODBMS may be a client of the ORB. The ODBMS may want to use the ORB services such as location and naming (for distributed name services) or may use the ORB in order to access other ODBMSs, thus allowing heterogeneous ODBMS access. Current ODBMSs provide object identifiers that work only within one vendor's products, sometimes only within one database. The ORB object references could serve as a common denominator that allows selected object references and invocations in an ODBMS to span database boundaries (via encapsulating ODBMS object identifiers within ORB object references).

B.4 ODBMS as an Object Manager

The ORB acts as a communication mechanism to provide distributed, transparent dispatching of requests to objects among applications and service providers. The ODBMS acts as manager of a collection of objects, most of which are not directly registered as objects to the ORB, some of which can be very small (fine-grained) application objects, and for which high-speed transparent distributed access must be supported.

If every ODBMS object that an application wanted to reference were individually registered with the ORB or if every request to those objects in the ODBMS went through the ORB Basic Object Adaptor, the overhead would be unacceptable. This is equivalent to saying that every test of a bit of data or change of an integer must invoke the overhead of an RPC mechanism. Instead, the application should have the flexibility to choose which objects and which granularities are in fact known to the ORB, when requests to those objects go through the ORB, and be able to change this choice from time to time.

To achieve this maximum flexibility, we specify that the ODBMS has the capability to manage objects unknown or known to the ORB, to register subspaces of object identifiers with the ORB (to allow the ORB to handle requests to all of the objects in an ODBMS without the registration of each individual object), and to provide direct access to the objects it manages. For the objects unknown to the ORB, this direct access is provided via an ORB request to a containing object (e.g., a database), which then makes those objects directly available to the application. This provides consistency with and participation in the ORB environment and still provides the ODBMS with the ability to move objects around the distributed environment, cache them as appropriate, and provide efficient access.

For objects that the ODBMS has registered with the ORB, it may choose either to let requests to them execute the normal ORB mechanism or request from the ORB that any requests to those objects be passed to the ODBMS, perhaps for some period of time. Requests to such objects, whether through the ORB or directly to the ODBMS, must produce the same effect and be compatible with other users employing both mechanisms. In this way the ODBMS can provide consistency with the ORB and still coordinate with direct object requests.

The currently adopted OMG CORBA document provides for normal object access via the Basic Object Adaptor (BOA). For complete generality, flexibility, and interoperability, it executes via an interprocess mechanism (RPC for short) for every dispatch of every method. An extension is the Library Object Adaptor (LOA) that allows direct considerably faster access to objects. After the first invocation (via the usual ORB mechanism), or through a compile-time optimization, a direct link is established to the object. Later access by the client to the object is then direct until the client notifies the ORB that it has released the object. We offer a new type of Object Adaptor, the Object Database Adaptor (ODA), to provide the ability to register a subspace of object identifiers and to allow access (including direct access) to the objects as if they had been individually registered.

The ODA provides a mechanism to register a subspace of object identifiers with the ORB rather than having to register all objects in the ODBMS. From the client's point of view, the objects in the registered subspace appear just as any other ORB-accessible objects, with the same interface. The ODA should allow for the use of direct access (as in the LOA) to improve the performance of ORB/ODBMS applications.

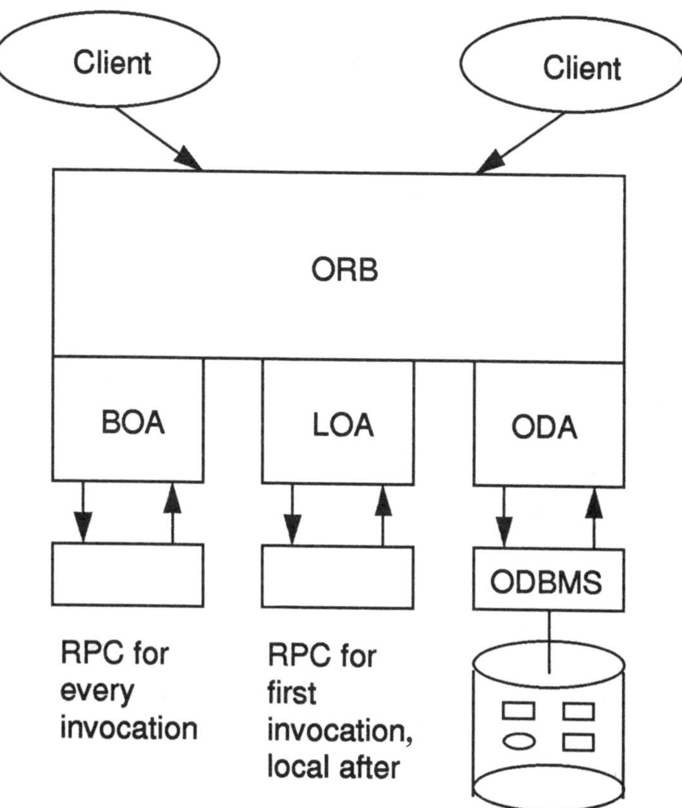

Figure B-1. ODBMS as Object Manager in OMG ORB Architecture

Appendix C

C++ Language Extensions

C.1 Introduction

The purpose of this appendix is to consider some problems in the current definition of C++ that are of interest to ODMG. In some cases the problem is clear, and a straightforward language extension proposal can be made to address it. In other cases the problem can only be stated in general terms with suggested directions for possible solutions and further investigations.

ODMG has as a goal the active investigation of C++ language design and standards issues that impact the C++ language interface to object database management systems. The group plans to participate in and submit concrete proposals to standards bodies such as ANSI that will make the language more useful to the object database development community.

C.2 ODL/OML and C++ Standards Compliance

The ODMG should ensure that all ODL/OML notations are conforming extensions to the C++ language. Some CASE environments, for example, accept conforming extensions but will report errors on nonconforming ones. It is important that existing CASE tools remain useful when developing and browsing ODL/OML class definitions and programs.

C.3 Object Views and Overloading Operator "dot"

A capability available in relational databases, but not available in object databases based on current C++ syntax, is the ability to create logical "views" of data. In the relational model, views are relations based on projections and joins of other relations. In an object model, views are classes based on selected member fields or combinations of member fields from other classes. As with the relational model, member fields of a view may be computed (intentional) rather than stored (extensional).

ANSI document X3J16/92-0048 proposes an extension to the C++ standard for overloading the . operator. If this proposal were accepted, it would be possible to provide access functions that behave as though they are stored fields in an object. For example,

```
class MyClass {
public:
    int operator . value() { ... }
```

```
}
MyClass mc;
int my_value = mc.value;          // Calls MyClass::operator.value()
```

Here is an example of a view class that joins the member fields of two other classes:

```
class First{
    int first_value;
    ...
};

class Second {
    int second_value;
    ...
};
class View12 {
    Ref<First> first_ref;
    Ref<Second> second_ref;
public:
    int first_value() { return first_ref->first_value; }
    int second_value() { return second_ref->second_value; }
    ...
};
```

C.4 Object Update and Overloading l-values/r-values

Database operations that modify database values need to notify the database system that the object has been modified so that the system will write the object to disk. Relying on the programmer to call a mark_modified() member function whenever a database object is modified introduces the possibility of corruption if the function is not called and the object is consequently not written back to disk.

ANSI document X3J16/92-0048 proposes a further extension to the C++ standard to provide different behavior for l-value and r-value usage of the . and [] operators. This proposal also makes use of the overloaded '.' proposal in the same document. The function-id of the r-value operator remains as it is in the current standard. The function-id of the l-value operator would become the function-id of the r-value operator followed by a modifier for the following operations:

```
= += -= *= /= %= ^= &= |= <<= >>= ++ --
```

Overloading the . and [] operators of a persistent class would allow the ODMG C++ interface to provide automatic update notification to the database system, removing the responsibility from the programmer and eliminating a troublesome source of data corruption. For example,

```
persistent class MyClass {
public:
    int &operator .= value(const int new_value) {
        value = new_value;    // should not call .= value function!!
        mark_modified() ;
        return value;
    }
    ...
};
```

C.5 Relationships and Overloaded Operator->

The C++ language definition needs to clarify the behavior of temporary values and the overloaded -> operator. The clarification could be especially important for ODMG C++ code for follows relationships.

To see the problem, consider the following class declarations:

```
class First{
    Ref< Ref<Second> > toSecond inverse toFirst;
    ...
};


class Second {
    int i;
    Set< Ref<First> > toFirst inverse toSecond;
    ...
};
```

The following code assigns the value 7 to member i in class Second by following the relationship from class First:

```
Ref<First> firstRef;

firstRef->toSecond.get(n)->i = 7; // wrong: relies on life time of
                                  // temporary returned by toSecond()
```

This example works in cfront-based translators but may not for other C++ translators if the get() member function returns a Ref<Second> by value. The problem is that the example relies on the lifetime of the temporary returned by the toSecond.get() relationship method in class First. The temporary Ref to class Second may be deallocated before the assignment operator is executed, resulting in a runtime error that is hard to detect.

Section 13.4.6, "Class Member Access," in Stroustrup[1], says:

> Class member access using ->
>
> primary-expression -> primary-expression
>
> is considered a unary operator. An expression x->m is interpreted as
>
> (x.operator->())->m
>
> for a class object x.

Stroustrup then goes on to show an example of smart pointers. ODMG Refs are smart pointers of this kind, but the example is too simple to motivate the proposed change. In this case, if x is a temporary, we need x to survive long enough to evaluate the reference to m. The definition of -> as a unary operator makes this impossible to guarantee.

The C++ standard allows aggressive management of temporary objects in order to allow a compiler to optimize the code it generates. More recent C++ compilers delete temporary objects as soon as possible. This approach differs from the less aggressive temporary management used by AT&T cfront-based translators that wait until the end of the statement before deleting temporary objects. Relying on the way cfront manages temporaries can lead to coding errors that are hard to detect on non-cfront-based ANSI C++ compilers.

To make overloaded -> safe for use in following relationships, the C++ standard must clearly state that primary expression x must retain temporaries generated by evaluating x until after the entire m field reference has been evaluated, in the same way as the postfix operator . does in the expression x.n. This behavior is important to ODMG's C++ binding because relationship member functions can return Refs by value, and the Ref returned by the member function must not be destroyed until after the overloaded Ref class operator->() has done its job.

C.6 Object References and Pointers as First-Class Types

Refs serve the same role in databases as pointers do in memory. C++ currently lacks features that would allow Refs or other storage references to be handled with the same syntax and operations as memory pointers. It seems most consistent with the C++ design philosophy to consider how the language could be used to provide this capability.

C++ pointers can be thought of as simple objects that have no constructors or destructors and have a single storage cell for a memory address. It would be useful to consider a more general notion of a storage reference class that can have constructors, destruc-

---

1. Stroustrup, B. *The C++ Programming Language, Second Edition*, Addison Wesley Publishing Company, 1991.

tors, and additional operators. C++ memory pointers are a simple derived class of this storage descriptor class.

A more interesting derived class is one that refers to database objects. A database reference class holds the address of an object in the database, and may provide additional operations such as pinning the object in physical memory for a period of time. Other features could be added to other database reference-derived classes, such as maintaining reference counts, caching the memory pointer, and incrementing/decrementing pin counts as database reference objects are constructed/destructed or database objects are assigned.

The following sections note some of the extensions and problems that come up in the current C++ definition of this idea. These are simply points for thought, rather than fully fleshed out extension proposals. Much more language design work and a reference implementation to test the design are required before a concrete extension proposal can be made. Also note that there may be approaches other than this general one that would satisfy the goal of treating Refs more like memory pointers in C++.

C.6.1 Declaration

A way to declare a storage reference class must be provided for any object class. For example,

```
class MyClass { ... };
class MyClass * { ... };            // Storage reference class for MyClass
```

The storage reference class declaration must be available to all compilation units where the referenced class is declared. If no storage reference class is declared, a default one is provided that acts like the current memory pointer.

Defining an instance of a storage reference object uses the same syntax as pointer definition:

```
MyClass *aClass;
```

and the reference class object can be initialized using the same syntax as initialization for any other object.

C.6.2 Size of Storage Reference Object

Since the size of a storage reference object is arbitrary, the declaration of a storage reference object must always be available wherever the size of a storage reference object is needed, such as at allocation. Since pointers to objects are the same size in C++, this is a more restrictive requirement than is imposed by the current standard. However, this restriction is not in conflict with the standard because if the user declares no storage reference class, the size of the default storage reference object (i.e., a pointer) is assumed. Also note that pointers to strings and functions must already be declared as such because they are of different storage classes and may even be different sizes than a normal pointer.

C.6.3 The Problem of Void*

There is a special problem with the current definition of void*, which is defined to be the union of object, function, and string pointer types. The problem is that a void* can hold any pointer but will not in general be large enough to hold an arbitrary storage reference. There may be some ways to fit both the spirit and the practice of the current implementation, but some careful language design work will be required to produce a conforming interpretation of void*.

C.6.4 Dynamic Allocation and Deallocation

When objects of a class are allocated dynamically, the new operator returns a storage reference object as its result. The new storage reference object can be copied using the normal assignment operator:

```
MyClass *aClass = (MyClass *) new (MyClass);// new() creates object and
                                            // returns storage reference
```

The delete operator frees the storage referred to by a storage reference:

```
delete aClass;                              // frees referenced object
```

C.6.5 Other Operations on Storage References

Certain operations defined for C++ pointers are not predefined or are required to be defined on storage references. For example, pointer arithmetic may or may not make sense for a pointer reference. The class definition of a storage reference is responsible for defining the meaning of these operations. If the operations are defined, they should follow analogous rules to operations already defined on standard pointers.

C.7 Heterogeneity and Tagging Unions

Unions in database objects pose a particular problem for database systems that support heterogeneous access to objects. An object created on one machine architecture must be readable on a machine with another architecture. Consider the following example:

```
persistent class MyClass {
    union { int a;  double d; };
    ...
}
```

With no indication of which member is active, there is no way the persistent object storage can be sensibly converted for the current architecture.

One solution to this problem is to force a tag into the union that an architecture conversion routine of the database system can use to guide the conversion. One possible method for hiding a tag relies on overloading the . operator and providing operators for l-values to track which member is active (based on assignments or other usages).

The problem of unions and heterogeneity will require more investigation to determine whether a language extension would be useful and what that extension would do.

Index

D

E

F

G

H

I

K

L

M

N

O

P

Q

R

S

T

U

V

X